Seasoned Greetings

By

Tony Cobourn

Sharon + Spence
Now you will know the
dirty little secrets that
led to the couple you have
now befriended -
Tony

Seasoned Greetings
by Tony Cobourn

Printed in the United States of America

ISBN 1-594670-16-1

Introduction

"Aaaarrrghh!"

That was our standard response when the Dreaded Christmas Letters (DCL's) began to arrive in mid-December. The letters came folded inside Christmas cards embossed with the names of the senders. They were addressed to "Dear Friends and Family." The only thing remotely personal was that they were stamped, not metered.

They fell into two categories:

A) Pretentious:

"Well, Michelle has really blossomed in her ballet group this year. She starred again in the Nutcracker. *Huge* article in the local paper!"

"We loved Barbados so much last year we just *had* to go back again in April – this time for a whole month! Bill and I sailed our new ketch all the way from the cottage in Newport. What an incredible adventure!! You *must* do it!!"

"And Creighton, of course, having received a National Merit Scholarship, enrolled at Dartmouth where, in addition to starting as quarterback, he edited the school newspaper (first time ever for a freshman!) and assisted with a microbiological research project that has been labeled 'Top Secret' by the government. My, we are so proud!!"

B) Boring:
"Melissa continues to work at Kodak. She still has her little
apartment on Oak Street, but got a new roommate in July."
"Dick continues to work at Xerox, where he continues in the
shipping department. In February he was named Employee
of the Month and received a $25 gift certificate. He contin-
ues to enjoy his work."
"The cat continues to cough up fur balls, the last one right in
the middle of bridge club. Imagine!"

Clearly, these correspondents, mostly friends of our parents at
that time, were already living lives far richer (or quieter) than we
had yet experienced. We were young and unworldly, with little
babies and big debts. What was there about cradle cap and croup
that is worthy of a Christmas Letter? Yet, if we wrote a DCL, how
soon might we become Pretentious? What if we only got to Boring?

Finally, after our youngest, Elizabeth, had celebrated her third
birthday with a giant cake (that her mother both baked and ate), we
decided to tell our story as it had been that year, not as we wished it
were or hoped it might some day be. "Stuff" was going on with us –
some funny, some poignant – but life was neither Pretentious nor
Boring. Our contemporary Christmas card recipients could relate to
our lives. They knew that when Jennifer, our oldest, was a baby, I
would come home from work to find a rainbow over her crib –
God's sign that her mother had not changed her since 11AM. They
knew that Andy, our second child, had thrown up his formula so
regularly and forcefully that Edith fed him over the sink, and that
every blouse she owned had a tan racing stripe down the back.

Our second move (out of six) with IBM prompted our surrender
to the DCL. With each relocation, our circle of correspondents grew
and our available time – with three children – diminished. No
longer able to pen leisurely notes as we sat sipping mulled cider in
our cozy breakfast nook, we succumbed.

And it was good.

We pledged to purge the Pretentious and ban the Boring. The
results were apparently rewarding enough that, years later, there are
still folks we haven't seen in ages who send Thanksgiving cards

begging us not to drop them from our Christmas list.

May you, dear reader, enjoy our family's growth as much as we did.

Acknowledgements

First, of course, I must acknowledge my family for their contributions – their behavior and misbehavior which provided the stories and for their forbearance in allowing me to tell them. Actually, their forbearance wasn't always automatic. When they were younger, they'd get halfway through a sentence and pause. "Oh, no, Dad's going to put that in the Christmas letter." As teenagers, they became a wealth of material, and their protests grew harsher: "Dad, if you put that in the Christmas letter, I'm going to … " ("What?" I'd think. "What are you going to do? Leave home? Hold your breath until I've finished paying for college?")

Edith was so convinced that she'd been maligned, she couldn't even read the drafts. Jennifer was happy to get an early copy so she could "tell me what parts I love and what parts I hate."

Despite these impediments, I finished the book.

I am particularly grateful to my editing group: Jody Vickery, Mike Miller, and the Comma-Nazi, Scotty Brewington. They reigned me in, let me go, brought me back, and when I was done (did I need to set that off with commas, Scotty?) the book was "all tightened up." If you end up not liking this book at all, I will be glad to provide you with their addresses and phone numbers.

But, before the editing group … way before…there was Dobie – Doris Vickery – the Baldwinsville, NY, high school English teacher who planted this writing seed in me and helped it to germinate. She praised my young creative efforts back in the late '50's, guiding gently, encouraging me to write and read and write some more. If you end up liking this book at all, give her lots of credit.

And if you had a teacher who planted a seed in you which bore fruit, *please* let him or her know how appreciative you are. That's a teacher's only true reward, you know – seeing a student's success and hearing him say, "Thanks."

A. D. Cobourn
Roswell, Georgia
December, 2002

The Cobourns
115 Riverglen Road
Liverpool, NY
Christmas, 1973

Ho Ho Ho and Ho,

OK. For those of you who recoil upon receiving cold, crass, creepy Christmas letters: read on. This will not bore you with trips to the Keys and country club gossip. This is REAL LIFE! Good old American black and white TV, not those Godless new color sets. Beer and pizza, not Brie and Chablis. And, it'll be a lot funnier than the Christmas greetings the Nixons send this year!

Actually, this letter is a calculated concession to my beloved wife's inability to write those folksy little Christmas card inserts anymore. Edith is overburdened with parental, ecological, and humanitarian projects.

All those time-consumers of hers demand some explanation. First, Edie has become chairman of the Kappa Kappa Gamma advisory board at Syracuse University. She is, in that lofty role, liaison between the old broads and the young hons, is on call 24 hours a day (usually at suppertime), and generally completes her projects and correspondence no later than 3:00 AM of the day they're due. Also interspersed in a typical week are tennis lessons, Junior League events, environmental group meetings, and upholstery classes. Whew!

I am also into Alumni Relations as president of the Delta Upsilon alumni council at Hamilton College. We have found that the generation gap is <u>real</u>, but can be spanned – like with the bridge over Lake Ponchartrain. At the other end is pot and free love. It's HELL to grow old!

At work, I am primarily involved with compensation and benefits, recruiting, and salary administration. You'll remember from last year that I transferred from IBM's Rochester branch office to get away from my boss, Attila the Hun, only to wind up in Syracuse working for his brother, Eddie the Hun. Far from a joyful career leap, this was a desperate lateral move to escape imminent death as a first-line manager – a sentence imposed by my boss, whose intellectual capacity barely exceeded that of a cherrystone clam. We lost money on the house, of course, and the IBM fire in Syracuse wasn't much better, at first, than the IBM frying pan in Rochester. Early this year, though, the new District Personnel Manager needed an assistant who had management experience. As the only one in the office with those qualifications, I grabbed at the chance. I think the personnel staff is my forte. We'll see. My free time is taken up with the church choir and Monday Night Football, both equally noble pursuits.

Jennifer has just turned nine and has become a swimming fanatic. Her interest began last summer at our community swim club, and she is now on the village team. We can't believe her dedication – she has even been willing to forego birthday parties for swim practice! She won a couple of meets in the breaststroke this summer. Jennifer is also active in Brownies, an interest surpassed only by having a friend stay overnight. Third graders are wonderful. They understand what you are talking about when you whisper and use big words, but they don't hear you when you ask them to wipe their feet. They can argue, but they can't spell. And they watch Sunrise Semester in the morning if cartoons aren't on yet.

Andy is just six and participates with me in Indian Guides. Unlike Scouts, Indian Guides includes all the fathers. The highlight of our fall season was a weekend outing in a local park where we slept in railroad cars, sharing and bonding and freezing. The adult bonding came undone when two of the fathers began snoring at 110 decibels. It's hard for an Indian to escape snoring in a Pullman. Anyway, I'll bet real Iroquois never slept in railroad cars.

Andy is now in first grade and is just learning to read and write. It's fun having him read us a few pages at night – we go upstairs right after dinner so he'll be done by 8:30. He, too, enjoyed swimming this summer, and both kids love to skate. We built a 20' X 40' rink in the back yard this winter. I was deeply involved in this activity. I froze but didn't bond. Here's how you build a rink: Dad sits outside for 11 hours filling it up, freezing his petuties off while the kids look out through the window of the toasty family room, calling out periodically to ask if he is done yet. It was an uneconomical family project, by the way: $83 for the materials and $17 gazillion for the water.

That leaves Elizabeth, whose greatest fault currently is that she never finishes her supper. We are puzzled about the origin of this trait as neither Edith nor I has missed many meals. Liz is three and will turn four in May, if we let her. We recently moved her in with Jennifer so Edie could have a sewing room. The result, of course, is that Edie has yet to sew a buttonhole, and Jennifer and Elizabeth stay awake talking until midnight.

We've settled into the Liverpool community and are actually liking it now. After several unhappy visits to Liverpool's Episcopal Church, we began attending the United Church of Christ in Bayberry. Its service doesn't seem drastically different, except that we no longer kneel, stand, genuflect, walk around, etc. One great thing about the church is that it's nearby, so I stroll over early every Sunday with banjo in hand (accompaniment for the folk hymns) and Edie dashes in with the kids in time to follow behind the processional, just the way she likes it!

Last Easter, long before 50 MPH speed limits, we enjoyed a 2400-mile, two-week trip visiting friends and relatives. I particularly enjoyed standing in line for four hours to see Ling-Ling and Tsing-Tsing at the Washington zoo. Come summer, with the gas shortage, we had to scale back the driving, so Edith signed us up for the annual 47-mile bike ride from Syracuse to Rome. She was told it was an almost totally flat route, following the Erie Canal towpath, with only one hill to climb. Since neither of us had ever done this sort of thing, we practiced by riding around the block a couple of times – me on my 3-speed English bike, and Edith on an old 1-speed Schwinn with the basket on the front for the newspapers.

Well, we faced the one hill (actually, the first hill) within 153 feet of the starting line. Naturally, we got off and walked our bikes up the hill, impeding the masses behind us on their 10-speeds. All we heard were 7,000 "Passing Lefts!" Within minutes we were at the back of the pack, struggling to stay ahead of the sag wagon. Two hours down the road, we began to see the early leaders returning from Rome! This was becoming an altogether depressing venture. But we made it, three hours later. I passed out and Edith cramped up. They loaded our bodies and our bikes into a bus and mercifully shipped us home. In less than a week the lactic acid dissipated and we could walk again. Maybe we'll watch next year's trek on TV.

Now, to be fair to Edith (a trait for which I am not famous) her environmental group won an award at the NY State Fair this summer for its Beaver Lake project. They brought inner city 4th and 5th graders to the Beaver Lake Nature Center in Baldwinsville last year, and guided them around the trails. Can you imagine Edith pointing out a cardinal in a conifer? She had to take a naturalist course in order to be a guide. She thinks it would be easier to be a docent at Cooperstown. Their current project is to take nature to the kids by means of an "Earth Bus" – a mobile center to be used on inner-city school grounds.

Her role in undergraduate relations at Syracuse U. needs some further clarification. Two years ago, if anyone had forecast her doing, much less liking, this advisory job, she would have responded, "NO WAY!!!" (Elizabeth's favorite retort). It really is fun for her, though, because she is able to converse periodically with someone older than nine.

Business and parenting aside, Edith has a newfound love of the ocean. In August, she took the children to visit her sister, Martha, who lives on the Jersey shore. I was left home to paint the house – a mixed blessing indeed: glad for the quiet, but dismayed by the terrible price in scraping and caulking. Oh well, they were only to be gone three days. With ideal weather and water conditions, however, they ended up staying two weeks. Edie did phone home occasionally with whiny variations on:

> "Oh, Tony, it's so great here, do you mind if we stay
> just a few more days?"
> "No," I'd reply, "the cedar-shake shingles sucked up
> the first three coats so I need to paint it again
> anyway."

Our kids had never seen the ocean, but the water was warm and mostly calm, so two out of three of them adapted quickly. Jennifer was first in the surf. Andy was happy to wade and collect crab claws, now his favorite thing. Once he saw a crab claw, he dropped dinosaurs like a bad habit. Elizabeth wouldn't even get her toes wet until the second week, so she was no worry. They found lots to do at the seashore – like collecting things. For our kids, anything is collectible. Jennifer found a huge starfish which they kept for a few days as a pet. After it died, they tried to dry it in the sun. The odor soon prompted a burial at sea. Edie hummed the Navy Hymn.

Another great pastime for them was sitting on the boardwalk looking at the weirdos. Kids got a little bored with that after a while, but not Martha and Edith. They explored a good length of the Jersey shore – from the castle-like mansions of Monmouth to the cottages of Ocean Grove, a very sheltered Methodist community, and then all the way down to Point Pleasant.

Martha sent them home with Friendly, a "free" kitten – reminding me of the "free" tropical fish my sister once gave us which required $150 in paraphernalia. Anyway, one could not ask for a nicer cat than Friendly, meaning that Friendly stays out of my way.

Martha is coming for Christmas, and we'll probably greet her with a blizzard. Haven't had much snow yet, so we are due. It has been a little brisk, though, with the thermostat at 68°. This patriotism stuff during the fuel crisis is a real sacrifice!

Hope you have a wonderful Christmas season and a happy New Year,

The Cobourns
9625 North Pond Circle
Roswell, GA 30076
Christmas, 1974

Merry Christmas from Dixie,

I had spent thirty-three+ years in the north, and didn't know any better. I knew folks from Syracuse who vacationed in Florida and Louisiana, but I was unaware that actual people lived there! All that changed when IBM announced its reorganization du jour and closed the District Office in Syracuse. Typically zealous about taking care of its employees, IBM assured us all jobs somewhere. I was offered a promotion to Boston, but opted instead for a lateral move to the new General Systems Division headquarters in Atlanta where I joined the Employee Relations staff. GSD manufactures and sells IBM's small computers. The division's newness makes the staff work exciting – an altogether wonderful job in a location <u>significantly</u> less expensive than Boston. It's significantly less expensive than Syracuse, too. The property, sales, and state income tax rates are one-fourth what they were in New York State! Now that we're here, though, don't ya'll follow us down and screw things up.

Another feature unique to the South is what the locals call "sunshine." For those of you receiving this in Rochester or Buffalo, "sunshine" comes from something called a "sun." It is a big bright ball of burning gasses, apparently located at the center of our solar system, which you can see here in the sky almost every day. It must be very hot, because it keeps away things like snow. No one is sure why God would grace the South with "sun" when perfectly worthy and righteous people in Watertown can still see their breath on Memorial Day.

I started the new job right after the first of the year, commuting home on the weekends and leaving Edie to keep the driveway shoveled so realtors could come in and criticize our house. It turns out Syracuse had a record 160" of snow last winter. Pray for Edith's back. It went out one day and never returned. Never called.

Never wrote. She borrowed a spare one from a neighbor in February and came to Atlanta to house hunt. Edie got off the plane in her genuine simulated muskrat coat, making it easy for me to pick her out of the crowd of those more familiar with Georgia. "Take that <u>stupid</u> coat off!" I explained, "so we can look for houses without being taken for carpetbaggers!"

We found a place in Martins Landing, a development near the village of Roswell, 15 miles north of Atlanta. Subdivision names in the south are often pretentious, as if to suggest roots in Wales or the Virginia Colony – like "Olde Towne Parc," which craftily blends England and, I guess, France. Part of Martins Landing borders the Chattahoochee River, but it is unclear that anyone named Martin ever landed here. I think a drunken fisherman named Marty fell out of his raft and beached a couple of years ago, but I don't know if that counts.

Our section of the subdivision was only recently built, meaning all the neighbors are new to one another, and seek each other out first to form friendships. There are lots of kids nearby who are the same ages as ours, so the move has been relatively smooth. Young Gardner Holden Randall, Jr. next door and Bret Ciaramella across the street have provided an instant transition for Andy. Bart Randall and Dana Ciaramella are Liz's age. Four year-olds are feistier than seven year-olds. Liz came in crying the other day after having been disciplined by Dana's mother.

"What did you do, Liz?" we said.

"Well, I thlapped Dana'th faith. REAL hard!"

"Oh dear, why did you do that?"

"Becauth she called me fart-faith thirty-theven timthe."

While working here before the move, I bought tickets for the family to the Atlanta Braves' opening game on April 7. None of the kids had ever seen a major league game, so I was sure this would be a great welcome to our new city. It turned out to be a greater welcome than I could have imagined. April 7 was the game in which Hank Aaron hit his 715th home run! Wow! 56,000 fans screaming and hugging and spilling beer on each other. After about 20 minutes of this revelry, I noticed Jennifer had sat back in her seat and was crying. Thinking she'd gotten poked by an exuberant fan I said, "Jen, what's wrong, honey? Are you OK?" "Oh, Daddy," whimper, whimper, "I just feel so sorry for Babe Ruth."

My father's emphysema continued to worsen this fall, despite the warmer climate of Hendersonville, NC. He and mom have lived there since 1971, when his doctor told him he could no longer take another Syracuse winter. At least we are close enough again to visit from time to time. Every couple of months we take the kids up for a long, apartment-bound weekend. Mom and Dad aren't terribly adventuresome, but there are some neat things to do around Hendersonville. In the spring we took the kids to Sliding Rock, a shallow stream nearby with a smooth, slippery rock bottom – perfect for sliding on butt or belly for several hundred feet. During a fall visit Jennifer and I found our first bluegrass concert at the local high school: two generations of recent Yankees falling in love with honest country music. No pretense here in the Appalachians! We are blessed to be briefly free from the growing "sophistication" of Atlanta.

Dad died in November from a heart attack. That's how emphysema victims die; their lungs can no longer provide enough oxygen to the blood and the heart wears itself out. Mom had called the week before to say that he'd been hospitalized. I drove up immediately for what turned out to be my last visit with him. His breathing was very labored, and there was terror in his eyes. I'd never seen that before in my father, the strong, capable Syracuse China executive. We both knew his time was short but, of course, stoic pilgrims that we are, we didn't discuss such uncomfortable things as death or love. He died four days later.

One would think this might have been the catalyst for me to quit smoking. So far, it has only increased the depth of my guilt, abetted by the kids' shrill and insensitive warnings. Edie quit in 1971, but I admit I haven't had much success myself. Boy, this is hard!!

Speaking of Edie, she's begun seeking out extracurricular activities which offer respite from the three stooges (Curly, Moe, and Elizabeth). She attended her first Atlanta Junior League meeting in the fall. The hostess served Co' Cola in elegant stemware on filigreed silver trays. The topic for the morning was a proposal to move the meeting start time from 10:00AM to 10:30AM because the maids of so many of the Buckhead members could not bus in from the ghettoes of southwest Atlanta by 10. Edie thinks the Junior Leagues in Rochester and Syracuse were a little more externally focused. This may not become her principal activity.

Tennis may become her principal activity. There's a swim and tennis club in Martin's Landing, the River Club, and Edith has become an avid participant. Atlanta has an organization called ALTA (the Atlanta Lawn Tennis Association) which places its 20,000 members into leagues and divisions and levels. While most of the participants consider ALTA matches good fun and good exercise, some teams have rabies. We thought golfers were intense! The trophy is a plastic tag for your tennis bag which proclaims you won your division. Women, in particular, *kill* for these tags. Nirvana is having at least two tags, so they click together. When you walk onto the court and your opponent hears your "clickers," she is properly intimidated.

Before we close, let me introduce you to southern politics. You thought the big political story this year was Nixon's resignation. Not in Georgia. The big news is the governor's race. Jimmy Carter is in his last term. (First of all, most Georgia politicians have diminutive or hyphenated first names: Jimmy, Billy-Joe, etc. Not too many Chaunceys or Athertons here. Roswell's mayor is named "Pug.")

There are eight candidates for the Democratic primary – in effect, for the governorship. The top candidate is a former governor, the ever-popular Lester Maddox, whose most notable accomplishment so far has been riding a bicycle backwards on the Johnny Carson show. I've been to his restaurant where he sells clocks to "Wake Up America" to the scourge of the coloreds. He also sells axe handles in case you need one of those for whatever reason. Another notable prospect is J. B. Stoner, the lovely and talented candidate from Marietta, prime suspect, but so far unindicted, in several Alabama civil rights crimes.

Edie and I watched a local debate among these clowns. We were used to Bobby Kennedy and Averill Harriman and Nelson Rockefeller. J. B. Stoner described his platform as anti-ERA, "so's we won't have our womenfolk in the trenches with them

9

buck niggers." The TV moderator, John Pruitt, was speechless – couldn't think of a good follow-up question. I wonder if we click our heels three times we can return to upstate New York. Jacob Javits never looked so good.

So here we are in Georgia for Christmas. Looks like we'll have lots of material for next year's Christmas letter.

'Til then we hope you have a wonderful holiday,

The Cobourns
9625 North Pond Circle
Roswell, GA 30076
Christmas, 1975

Dear Folks,

We can hardly believe that this is just our second Christmas in Georgia. We had a sudden yearning recently for a 12-foot snow bank, but we've already gotten over it. Still, it doesn't seem quite right to be hanging a Christmas wreath in 70° weather. I had to mow the lawn during a warm spell last January. No need to winterize your mower around here. We hear there are flurries in the Tennessee mountains. Maybe it'll be on TV.

We have really "gotten into" the community this year. This is probably deliberate since none of us wants to leave – although Elizabeth does ask where we're going "when we get through with this house." I am heading up our homeowners' association and Edith has been working on the River Club pool and tennis board. Martin's Landing is a planned unit development like Reston, VA, in which all the residents own the common property. (Little did we know!) The developer is now activating a homeowner foundation which will administer the lake, pools, tennis courts, and green belts. It's almost as complex as setting up a village government, The area is beautiful, though, and we think it will certainly be worth the time and money.

Earlier this summer, we worked hard to get Martin's Landing annexed into the city of Roswell. It took a 60% approval by those who were both landowners and registered voters. Of course, no one was anxious to add Roswell city taxes to his county tax burden. The measure did pass, but in January we may face legislation from the state which would annex Roswell into the city of Atlanta!

This is an interesting issue for us. We've never before lived near a big, expensive city. We wanted to become a part of Roswell (a village, really: 5,000 people) because of the better local services. We are battling an Atlanta takeover because our money will drain into the bottomless inner city pit. Poor Atlanta can't sustain itself anymore, yet it has attractions and activities that make the surrounding areas viable. We hope we can figure it all out before we have another Detroit fifteen miles south of us.

Jennifer spent a week with my mother in North Carolina this summer. They had a great time together, and we're delighted Jennifer can cultivate that relationship. Jen is just old enough to help and Grammy just young enough to care. Too bad it's such a long distance, though, since Mom is the last living grandparent. My grandmother always used to have just enough dimes for the Skippy Ice Cream Man. And she'd spend hours with me at Thornden Park in Syracuse looking for four-leaf clovers. And she'd let me beat her at Canasta. And she'd let me stay up and listen to "The Shadow" and "The FBI in Peace and War" until 9:30 at night! I wonder if my mom and dad ever found out. Kids need a good balance between uptight parents and indulgent grandparents.

Edith went on a campout with Jennifer's scout troop this summer – Edie's first tenting since childhood – with 75° weather in early November! Friday night, needing to establish "relationships" with the other two helping mothers, she got little or no sleep. Saturday, when the camp leader announced, "Free time!," the mothers sprinted to their tents and dove into their sleeping bags for a quick 20 winks. Saturday night, nothing could have kept her awake. Back home Sunday, she was zonked. Edith and I are OLD scouts and to us the simple life is exhausting. It's easier to buy Moon Pies than to make S'mores, but the ambiance isn't quite the same.

Nevertheless, after Jennifer's campout, Andy decided the best way to celebrate his eighth birthday (November 19) was to go camping with his father. We borrowed a tent and drove about an hour north to Lake Lanier. We fished, hiked, chopped wood, and bonded all day Saturday. All was well with the woodsmen until, as we cooked supper, the sun went down and the temperature dropped to 35°. When our lantern wouldn't work, we crawled into our sleeping bags at 6:45 PM! That night, the rain (yes, of course it rained) turned to snow. When we awoke to only the second snowfall in Atlanta in two years, we decided on a McDonald's breakfast, dressed quickly, broke camp, and were home by 9:15. Gardner Holden Randall, Sr., our super-macho submariner entrepreneurial

Eagle Scout rugby-playing neighbor with an Oklahoma EE and a Stanford MBA, won the betting pool. He had 9:20. Edie had hoped we'd stay out 'til Monday afternoon.

After swim team ended this summer, Andy went into the hospital to have a birthmark removed from his leg. It required a skin graft, 2 1/2 weeks of keeping the leg elevated, and frequent trips to the doctor to change the dressings, remove the stitches, etc. He was in the hospital two nights. I took the first night when we watched TV and ate pizza until 11:00. I gave Edie the second night when Andy threw up from the anesthesia. We're all glad that's over! Andy was a good patient, I must say. The graft looks very lumpy, but we were told it would take 6 months or more to begin to look good.

Elizabeth, at 4 1/2, is in kindergarten (private, of course, since Georgia has no public ones). She's still her same old self: lovable and devilish. She plays a mean game of Concentration and beats her mother like a tom-tom. Liz's brain is uncluttered by the stuff that impairs Edie's thought processes. You can just see the scheming mind behind those sparkling eyes in Liz's school picture. Then she wakes with a smile, lisps a cheery morning greeting, and your suspicions melt away. May she never grow up.

I guess that's enough news from the South for this year.

Hope ya'll have a wonderful holiday season,

The Cobourns
9625 North Pond Circle
Roswell, GA 30076
Christmas, 1976

Christmas Greetings,

Ordinarily, revenge is not an appropriate topic for a Christmas letter. I had a scrumptious opportunity for revenge this year, but opted not to seize it. You Rochester correspondents remember my alleged fall from grace at IBM and banishment to Syracuse in 1971. I blew the whistle on my boss, Attila the Hun, after he delayed my annual performance appraisal by 28 months. He fixed <u>me</u> – gave me a low evaluation and told me I was not promotable. I appealed the appraisal but never heard from the Branch Manager, so I assumed he agreed with Attila. The only escape was a humiliating lateral move to the district office in Syracuse.

Two years later I discovered that the Branch Manager had never gotten my appeal! My boss apparently stuck the appraisal in my file without even showing it to him. That's why I never heard from him. I was seriously considering reporting this deception to the VP of Personnel in Armonk when I learned that Attila had himself been demoted for conducting personal business on company time. The revenge? I was asked last spring by the new Branch Manager in Rochester if I would consider returning as the Administration Manager (where I would now be Attila's boss)! Ah, the intrigues of corporate life. Do I get extra points for not exacting the revenge even though I relished the thought?

I awoke early one spring Saturday morning to the sound of frantic pounding on my front door. Assuming it was The Rapture, I fell to my knees. Then I realized it was only Gardner Holden Randall, Sr., my take-charge neighbor. Several weeks earlier we had *casually* discussed reseeding a green belt which ran between our properties. Since such projects take actual physical effort, I preferred to let the concept cure for a while before I considered committing myself to hard labor. Not Gardner Holden Randall, Sr. He had bought (not rented) a roto-tiller and was ready to go. Oh, and by the way, I owed him for half the price of the tiller. My drill sergeant in the army was more sensitive than my neighbor!

After an hour of roto-tilling, it was clear that the Georgia clay needed some sand. (I was tilling; he was helping me perfect my technique. Does this sound like a Mark Twain story line?) So Gardner Holden Randall, Sr. and I hijacked his wife's VW bus, put a tarp in the back, drove to the local gravel pit, opened the sunroof, and had them dump a couple of tons of sand into the vehicle. We drove home on the rims, spread the sand, and I was able to hone my roto-tilling abilities for the rest of the afternoon while Gardner Holden Randall, Sr. practiced his leadership skills. We received "Green Belt of the Month" from the Martin's Landing garden club, and Mrs. Gardner Holden Randall, Sr. never got the sand out of the sunroof tracks. She was not at all amused. For several months thereafter Gardner Holden Randall, Sr. was no longer in command in the bedroom.

Later in the spring we became really patriotic and spent a couple of weeks on our entry for the Roswell Bicentennial Youth Parade. At first Edith thought we would take the easy way out and decorate bikes in red, white, and blue crêpe paper. Then Gardner Holden Randall, Sr. came up with the idea of portraying the Battle of Ft. McHenry, during which Francis Scott Key wrote the "Star Spangled Banner." You are probably unaware that Edith was named "Miss Compulsively Ambitious" in the 1961 Miss Syracuse pageant. She signed up on the spot. And I, ruthlessly trained by IBM to know a good idea when I hear one, proclaimed, "That's it! We'll do it or die!"

We almost died. You would have been invited to the memorial service. We neighborhood parents and kids built a fort, complete with cannon, and British man o' wars (or is that "men o' war?" or the politically correct "people of conflict?") circling menacingly. Edith and a neighbor sat in the fort, which we rigged atop the Randall's gritty VW bus, and fired flour from the cannon (using bellows) at the children in the bicycle-driven man o' wars. And through the entire parade we had the Star Spangled Banner blasting over a speaker on the bus. Old Francis Scott would have been proud. Needless to say, we took first prize, 'cause everyone else decorated bikes in red, white, and blue crêpe paper!

Edie had another little traffic oopsie this summer. This is her third now, after she destroyed our first car by running into a lamp post in the A&P parking lot, and crippled our second (my cherished 1964 1/2 Mustang) by running over a bicycle in the Anderson's driveway. This time, she was turning onto the main road at the end of an exit ramp when a car broadsided her from the left. The cop cited her for failing to yield. Edie never saw the other car, even though she had stopped and looked carefully. It turns out her view to the left was impeded by a bridge support. The other guy was speeding off the opposite exit ramp, and she never had a chance. If he'd been going the speed limit, he'd have had plenty of time to slow down.

Edie fought the ticket of course. She revisited the scene of the crime and noted that his ramp had no Yield sign, although there was a 35 MPH sign posted. With the Georgia Drivers Manual as her reference, she calculated distances, skid marks, etc., put it all on a flip chart, and headed to court. The judge called the case; Edie unrolled her flip chart and motioned for the bailiff to hold it while she extended her pointer to begin the presentation. The judge was stunned, and quipped that she should be home tending babies and cooking dinner. **Whoah!!!** Get Gloria Steinham on the line! Wake up Susan B! Edie held the judge in contempt of court. In exchange for mercy, he dropped the case and apologized to women the world over. By the way, the state has since installed a stoplight at that ramp.

Andy's swimming career peaked briefly this year. He swam breaststroke on the 9-11 year-old boys medley relay team. They had blown away the competition all season and were the favorites in the city/county finals. By the end of the second leg, they were up by ten seconds. Then, tragedy! Andy's best friend, Gardner Holden Randall, Jr., swimming the butterfly, started off the block before Andy touched out. The team finished ahead by <u>a length and a half</u> but was disqualified. They had broken the old record by 26 seconds.

That lapse did not diminish Andy and Gardner's friendship, though. During the summer, they established a lucrative Japanese Beetle trap business. Our annual infestation guaranteed their financial success. Their inverted plastic milk jugs were not as elegant as the colorful store-bought traps, but our Martin's Landing neighbors were pleased to support the local economy.

We started a monthly Gourmet Dinner Club this fall with three other neighborhood couples. This is an awesome fellowship activity if you like to cook or eat or drink or all three. The designated chefs gather for cocktails the week before the dinner, decide on the menu (French, Greek Peasant, Inuit, etc.), and assign dishes to make. On the evening of the dinner, the host couple provides the booze and the kitchen.

We have had two particularly memorable gatherings already. The first was our Russian dinner. Russian food itself is not particularly appetizing unless you like old beets, but every course is served with a flavored vodka. Put a flavoring agent in a pint of vodka and leave it in the freezer overnight. We had lemon peel vodka with our bliny and caviar, peppercorn with the borscht, tea-flavored with the cucumber and sour cream salad, and cherry-flavored with the Chicken Kiev and grated potato pudding. By the time we got to the anise vodka and Charlotte Russe with raspberry purée, that Commie food was tasting pretty scrumptious. Now we know how the Russians got through the German siege in the winter of 1941.

The second great dinner was Southern. Gardner Holden Randall, Sr., a case of Bud, and I sat up all night roasting half a pig. We entertained our neighbors with his harmonica, my banjo, and increasingly loud and bawdy songs from our college days. The food was good – pulled pork, Brunswick stew, corn bread, and collards – but not as good as the preparation.

We celebrated yet another Halloween with carefully hand-made costumes – another Cobourn tradition. I went as Superman. Had to suck in my stomach at each house. It's hard to ask for a refill of your bourbon and soda when you're holding your breath. Andy was Spiderman thanks to dyed long johns, a mesh bag head, and a clever Magic Marker. Liz was a witch again, complete with wide-brimmed hat and missing teeth. Jen was a purple cat, whiskers, claws and all. We scored some big-time treats!

We hope you are treated well this Christmas season,

The Cobourns
9625 North Pond Circle
Roswell, GA 30076
Christmas, 1977

Happy Holidays,

This year, as always, we seem to be having one trauma after another: Edith's 35th birthday – half a lifetime! This one really paralyzed her. I guess she was too busy to notice when she turned 30, but 35 had her quivering in the corner until I made it all better with my typically sensitive counsel, "Get OVER it, Edith!". Then Elizabeth entered first grade, and Jennifer became a teenager. I'm reminded daily of Mark Twain's advice upon acquiring a teenager: "Put it in a barrel, nail the top shut, and feed it through the bung-hole. And when it turns 16, plug up the hole."

My mother had a stroke in June and was hospitalized for two months. Her friends kept her company during the week and we commuted 200 miles to North Carolina for nine straight weekends. Try this sometime with three young kids and a broken A/C unit in your car; it will test your family resolve. In August, her doctor said she could go home as long as we could find a 24-hour companion. Yeah, right. My sister, Margaret, came down for a month, then took her to Myrtle Beach for two weeks, where she and her husband, Jimmy, live. Then mom returned home to manage by herself. Not quite what the doctor had in mind. She still hasn't much use of her left arm, and she walks with a quad cane, but her progress is remarkable. That she is living independently is a great example of courage to us all.

While Margaret was tending to her nursing duties, we managed to spend a week at Hilton Head with the Franklins, good friends and neighbors here in Roswell. We shared a lovely house belonging to friends of theirs – a five-minute bike ride to the beach or fishing pier. The kids found the crabbing, shelling, sunning, and swimming excellent, and Elizabeth caught a three-pound flounder! We enjoyed mediocre tennis (except for the match we saw Stan Smith and Brian Gottfried play). We had a brief memorial service for Elvis one evening, then got right back to the cocktail hour. Sea Pines at Hilton Head is truly a fantasy world.

Our big spring trip (oh, how do we keep it up, this go-go-go?) was to Plains, Ga! As soon as Jimmy was inaugurated, I wanted to be the first kid in my neighborhood to go there. Not high on Edie's list of historical must-sees, ranking just above the Franklin Pierce library, but we made the three hour trek from Atlanta one Sunday morning. Within five minutes we had seen everything there is to see in Plains, including Billy's gas station, which looks as if it should have been condemned by the Georgia State Health Department. We had a gourmet lunch at Aunt Mae's sandwich shop and split. Seriously, it did make me appreciate what Carter has accomplished. Going from that nowhere town to the presidency is unbelievable.

Early spring and summer: Edith was swim team co-chairman of the Martin's Landing River Rats with a girl who had moved here from Pittsburgh. Since Pittsburgh is where Edie spent her youth (I told her she shouldn't have spent quite so much of it), they got along great. They were the only two non-working moms absent from the organizational meeting, so they were unanimously selected team leaders. They were commissioned to find the right body to fit into the right navy blue swim suit; then find all 115 little bodies a stroke to swim in each of seven Monday night swim meets. After that experience, Edie could have survived a year in the Hanoi Hilton without cracking.

I was the swim meet announcer – the one bright spot for me during those hectic evenings. One day, I know, swim meets will be over, and Edith and I may once again have lives. In the meantime, I attend faithfully every week, straight from work, in my mildewing suit, desperate for a parking spot, desperate for a beer. Usually Andy and Liz are in the first two events of the evening and Jennifer is in the last. Can't they schedule these things by family instead of by age group and stroke?

When swim season ended, four of us exhausted River Rats fathers treated ourselves to a guys only fishing trip to the Georgia coast. Gardner Holden Randall, Sr., Pete Franklin, Dave Crawford, and I trailered Gardner's boat down to the Two-Way Fish Camp north of Brunswick, dreaming of late night poker games, huge hauls of tuna and marlin, and big greasy breakfasts of bacon, fish, eggs, home fries, and beer. Rain was not included in our dreams. The first day, on our 27-mile journey out to the gulf stream, the rain and heavy seas took their toll. I have one picture of Pete Franklin smiling as we boarded. The other thirteen photos show him throwing up off the stern, port, aft, abaft, starboard, galley, and conning tower. "Keep your eye on the horizon," Gardner Holden Randall, Sr. advised him. Pete tried that. It only made him throw up horizontally instead of vertically.

Edith's Conservation Crusades have expanded beyond the Chattahoochee River. She has joined a group called SONAR (Save Our Natural.......whatever....) which is trying to get commercial developers in Roswell to preserve the trees on their properties and to encourage shop owners to design their storefronts in keeping with the town's historical image. They have succeeded through pure pressure. If you attend every city council meeting for three months, the mayor and councilmen will get so sick of you they will appoint your group to be a review committee for the zoning board.

Edie talked Jennifer into one more year of scouts – Cadettes: 7th through 9th graders. Jen agreed only if Edie would be the co-leader and only if she would keep Jen's membership a total secret from her friends. Juliette Low would have been so proud. Little did Edith know how much deceit this would involve. None of Jen's school buddies is a scout, so if friends call her while she's involved in a scout meeting or project, we make up little stories about where she is. Edith has threatened lately to put up a big sign in the front yard saying, "JENNIFER COBOURN IS A GIRL SCOUT!" Jen and Edie even went camping last spring with her scout troop – a fun and easy trip when everything has to be in your backpack. Jennifer still is a dedicated year-round swimmer, practicing four nights a week – 22 miles away.

Probably the most daring thing Edith has done in ages was to return to the Women's Work Force. Tennis ended in October, so she decided to see if the old S.U. fashion merchandising major was still employable. After completing the application for Christmas help at Rich's, a big department store here, she prayed for two days they wouldn't call her. They called her. Naturally ... they hire anything for Christmas help that breathes without a respirator. Now she had to break the news to the family. Yikes!!! I thought it was OK but the kids were not thrilled. Of course, they weren't going to miss *her* a lot – just her services.

Well, she started on October 31, assigned to the china and crystal department. By the second day she had a migraine headache and almost threw up in a Waterford bowl – a humbling experience at slave wages. After two months on the job, though, she does like the department and has only broken five pieces of crystal! They promoted her from slave to serf so they could more quickly recover the damages from her pay.

Report Cards: Elizabeth managed all B's (and 11 N's – needs improvement); a mixed report in second grade. She must be a victim of the dreaded under-achievement gene that curses the Cobourn family. Andy's academic career seems to have hit a new low in fifth grade. At a Cub Scout pack meeting recently, as Andy was getting his Citizenship Award, Edith whispered to a friend, "There stands Andy, looking handsome in his Webelos uniform, dripping with achievements, and today he brought home the WORST report card he has ever had!" The friend quipped, "Oh, you want both a good citizen and a smart student?" Jennifer is doing SUPER in 7th grade. One out of three ain't bad.

Almost forgot to tell you about our great Winter Wonderland here last year! For a week in January, the temperatures hovered around 30° and it snowed. The pond by our river froze and we were skating every minute for the two and one-half days it lasted. Best skating I've ever seen – not too cold, and the ice as smooth as a baby's butt. The kids borrowed skates from adult Yankee neighbors with small feet. The native Southerners thought it was too dangerous to skate, but they came and took pictures!

Ice-skating, by the way, is not the South's best-known sport. In fact, when the Atlanta Flames hockey team opened its first game here against the Minnesota North Stars, the fans cheered whenever anything exciting happened that they didn't understand. They erupted in the opening minute when one of the North Stars, with no one to pass to, dumped the puck into the Atlanta end, and the goalie casually deflected it to a defenseman. A "**SAVE!!!**" The Omni was pandemonium! The players stopped and looked up into the stands, thinking a riot had broken out and evacuation was imminent.

In closing, not to make you all jealous during this busy holiday season, but even though Edie's Christmas shopping, cards, etc., are not complete, her grocery coupons are all in order – alphabetically within category. I threatened to call the home and have them come for her, but she thinks order and neatness are important. I think she needs to get out more.

If you need to get out more, ya'll come see us, ya' heah?

The Cobourns
403 Pine Creek Road
Exton, PA 19341
Christmas, 1978

Christmas Cheer,

Well, here we are again; another year, another city. Who would have ever thought it would be Philadelphia? Don't say it. We've heard them all:

"On the whole, I'd rather be in Philadelphia."

"I spent a week there one day."

"Downtown Philadelphia has all the charm of Buffalo, with none of its socially redeeming significance."

Et cetera.

It was terribly hard for the family to leave Atlanta, but, as all devoted wives and children must do when "Daddy" gets a wonderful job opportunity, it is Whither Thou Goest. I guess if you're not looking forward to moving, it is only fitting that you get a crummy mover. We are still trying to think of something they did right. Unloading us at midnight certainly wasn't right. Losing a cushion to our couch was not right. Tearing the exhaust system out of the bottom of our car was downright mean-spirited. I know we need equal opportunity for the handicapped, but this was ridiculous.

We said "Bye, y'all" to Georgia at the end of the school year and headed north to spend quality time getting reacquainted with each other. I was busy learning my new job as Regional Personnel Manager. Edie's reacquaintance with the kids didn't take long. After three days, they had nothing more to say to one another, so they began marathon Monopoly games, interrupted only by the occasional unpacking of a box.

The first thing we did when the movers left was to hop in the car and drive to Central New York for my 20th high school reunion. Haven't missed one yet. Mary Pat Edmunds, the first girl in the class to get breasts (7th grade) still looks great! Three and a half marriages have not yet taken their toll. Nan Johnstone got her usual award for having the oldest child; Nan, the girl who couldn't say no. Based on Nan's reaction to the recognition this time, though, the charm of the award may be wearing off. Halfway through the cocktail hour Archie Armistead stood up and encouraged us to get right with God. He offered to save us all on the spot, but nobody responded to the altar call. Several alumni rushed to the bar, though, thinking Archie had announced the *last* call. Later we transferred Archie to the class of '59 for cash and a future draft choice.

Back home, we settled s-l-o-w-l-y into our first brand-new house. We've moved into another brand-new development, Pine Creek Valley, in Exton, PA, a few miles beyond Philadelphia's Main Line. I was traveling a lot, so Edie was left to deal with the builder, Ray Charles, and his ten blind mice. Edith couldn't have made it through all those hassles without a copy of Erma Bombeck's "The Grass Is Always Greener ... " constantly within reach.

Naturally, we found a swim team for the kids the day we closed on the house. That kept everybody busy and allowed us to escape the re-construction and clean-up crews for most of the summer. It's hard to believe now, looking down the street at all the festive Christmas decorations, that six months ago we were the Pine Creek Pioneers, bouncing over unpaved road to no driveway, slogging through our mud yard to "Home Sweet Home."

Actually, there *was* a problem with the house. Two months before we closed, a deranged environmentalist and his gasoline can toured the subdivision in hopes of reversing the desecration of the land he used to hunt. The house next door was burned to the ground. Luckily, by the time he got to our place, the few dribbles of gas he had left caused only minor damage.

The house itself, we're crazy about. (Oh, jeez, I'm starting to talk Pennsylvania Dutch!) The neighborhood is very friendly, and the only thing we lack is a playmate for Elizabeth. Jennifer, about whom we were most worried, has a best buddy already – same age, recent California transplant, right next door. Thank God for Gwen.

The woods at the back of the lot are a mixed bag. Deer still graze there and the privacy is a blessing, but the poison ivy thrives. Edie and I are now both allergic, but Andy has become the most susceptible. He was so swollen and blistered with the last dose that he needed a cortisone shot. We thought about painting him green and sending him out Halloweening as The Hulk. Andy failed to see the humor.

Since my new region is large, I bought a new car for the business travel. For a long time I was successful in keeping little kids' muddy footprints and mommy's Twinkie wrappers and half-filled coffee mugs out of my sacred vehicle. This obsessive protectionism vanishes, though, once Edith has christened a new car. This time she christened it with her very own vehicle, backing the wagon out of the garage into the Toyota. Well, hey, it's just a car. (***Now***, it's just a car; before it was a noble, pristine chariot.)

It turns out, the disparagement notwithstanding, that Philadelphia is a great city. It was cleaned up a lot for the bicentennial and, for the most part, remains attractive. There's a lot of row house renovation and new construction down by the river, outstanding foodstuffs in the Italian market, great historical sights, of course, plus Rocky's museum steps. Edith is the tour guide and makes sure we see all there is to see. Last fall, while waiting in line to view the Liberty Bell with the Matthaidesses, who are still in their same house in Rochester from 1967, I remarked on how shallow a life they would have led had they not had gypsies like us to visit. After the downtown history we took them to Longwood Gardens, the Wyeth museum at Chadds Ford, and finished up with Amish country on the way back from Gettysburg!

I think Jen and Andy had a great desire to make Georgia schools look good. They have really cracked the books this year, and their efforts have paid off. Jennifer made the 8th Grade Honor Roll. We promised we wouldn't brag like this but it is, after all, a Christmas letter. Edith and I were so stunned we immediately bought her something – an unacceptably dangerous precedent for otherwise prudent parents. We hope she settles back into mediocrity quickly so we can afford to keep her through high school.

Andy, too, seems highly motivated in school this year, and it has nothing to do with our threatening to put him back in 5th grade. He was reluctant to join a scout troop, but with a little encouragement (same enlightened techniques which now prompt him to do homework), he signed up. Edie didn't devote two years of her life as a Cub Scout den mother for nothing! Andy is not showing the same zeal in practicing the guitar he bought himself this summer. He's had two months of lessons from a man who looks absolutely Cro-Magnon, and whose music tastes also run to that era. If only Andy could grow hair on his fingers I bet the cro-guy would make him a protégée. Meanwhile, Andy prefers "Stairway to Heaven" to the scales.

The rest of the family is also expressing itself musically this year: Liz and I in our respective church choirs, Jennifer in the Jr. High Chorus, and Edie in the "Larks," a group of twelve Philadelphia Junior Leaguers who sing twice a month at homes for the elderly. They started out performing at schools, but quickly discovered the audiences could actually hear them, so they discreetly switched to nursing homes. Without a piano in the house, Edith has had trouble practicing the music. I came home one night to find her attempting "The Messiah" on the pitch pipe. So Edith, ever the bold and resourceful musician, found kids' activities in areas with nearby piano stores. She remembered this tactic from when the kids were toddlers, and she had to learn where all the public restrooms were.

We are all geared up for northern winters again: snow tires, sleds, boots, etc. An early snowfall is picturesque, but the spirituality of that experience may soon wear off. It is, however, fun for Edie to be in the north country with kids who can dress themselves. All she has to do on snow days is man the dryer. Jennifer has joined the school ski team. We applaud her ambition and dread the cost, finally understanding the sound of one hand clapping.

We're not trying to discourage guests, but visiting relatives have been put to work at our new home. My sister, Margaret, arrived from Virginia to find herself thrust into painting the living room. Edith's sister, Martha, whom Edie had not seen in four years, came over to help her build a wall next to the driveway. They hauled so many rocks the United Mine Workers tried to organize them. Martha lives on the Jersey shore, only 2 1/2 hours away now, so we hope we'll get to see her more often. Close relatives are scarce in this family. Each of us has only one sibling and neither has children, so we have one grammy (my mother) and two aunts. Mom and Martha will join us for Christmas.

May God bless your holidays, too,

The Cobourns
403 Pine Creek Road
Exton, PA 19341
Christmas, 1979

Merry Christmas to all,

We're about to spend our second Christmas in Pennsylvania. The year began strangely. We went to the Mummers parade in downtown Philly. You've all seen it on TV: gorgeous costumes, string bands, crazy floats, cheerful crowds. It ain't the same live and in color, boys and girls. The real Mummers parade is drag queens and freaks and drunks – lots of knee-walkin' drunks. We are told on TV that they are "strutting." Actually, they are staggering. The Mummers start getting into it the night before as they finish up their floats and routines. By parade time, they are so blitzed all they can do is mum. ("Mum" is an 18th Century American word meaning "to throw up on the observer of a parade.")

After cleaning up, it was time to return to work the next day. My job as Personnel Manager for the Mid-Atlantic Region is probably the best assignment I've ever had with IBM. The region includes upstate New York, central and eastern Pennsylvania, New Jersey, Maryland, Delaware, and Washington, D.C. I do some traveling, but relatively few nights are spent away from home. My job is a pretty independent one and the region reliably meets its objectives so we don't have a lot of "help" from Division Headquarters. The regional assignment is a "full service" personnel function – recruiter training, compensation, employee relations, management training, etc. – and is both more challenging and more rewarding than the narrower staff functions at headquarters in Atlanta.

The job was especially challenging during the Three Mile Island disaster this year. Harrisburg is about 65 miles east of us. Shortly after the news broke, we began getting calls from our customer engineers. "Hey, I gotta get my wife and kids outta here! I'll call you when I get to my mother-in-law's in Scranton!" Click. This understandable edginess did not go away for a while, despite the government assurances that "everything was safe." We have computers installed at the reactor site and we prayed that none of them would require a service call.

Far from Three Mile Island, my mother is still living alone in her apartment in Hendersonville, NC. Mom has never driven a car – the result, apparently, of a very scary ride with her brother back in Camden, NY, in the early 20's. I could never survive without the freedom to get out, but she manages just fine. Of course, we are not as close to North Carolina as we were in Atlanta, necessitating an elaborate routine for Christmas visits. Mom, that fearful adventurer, hates air travel. So I have to fly from Philadelphia to Washington to Asheville, rent a car, pick her up, and retrace that route with her to Philly, fighting gangrene in my hand from takeoff to landing as she clutches my wrist. We reverse the process a few days before the New Year. Expensive little trip. Driving from Atlanta to Hendersonville to get her for a holiday was easier. Plus, I got to load up on cigarettes at $3.50 a carton.

Edie and I made the kids' Halloween costumes again this year. Andy was Bigfoot and the girls were dice. This continues to be a regular family tradition since our Syracuse days when we started out with Andy as Spiderman, Jen as a cat, and Liz as a witch (type-casting). That Halloween we had eleven inches of snow. The neighbors gave out candy to the kids and highballs to their parental escorts. Well, with all the effort required to hand make the outfits, we *deserve* our fill of candy and booze. For example, Andy's Jaws costume last year was a serious undertaking – finding gray material for the body (sharkskin?), sewing on fins, attaching a domed plastic ice bucket for the head, cutting the styrofoam teeth.....I'm exhausted just by the memory of it. But the kids love the attention their unique costumes bring. Try it some year. You might even get a free bourbon refill.

Shortly after the new year, Edith went for her Pennsylvania driver's license. We'd lived here since June; maybe she thought my job came with a 6-month probationary period. She drove to the license bureau on Monday, January 29th, her birthday and the day her Georgia license expired. She studied the manual in the car on the way. Guess which day the Pennsylvania license bureaus are closed?

Back the next day; birthday now passed; demoted to a permit and now must get a physical and take a road test; drove home (illegally) to make doctor's appointment. Had physical the next day; back to license bureau; insurance cards no good. Had them re-issued for Pennsylvania. Back again. Almost through – oops – forgot her damn birth certificate. NUTS! Next day, inspection sticker expired. Drove home (illegally) and had a drink. Edie thinks nomads like us are entitled to two things: a nationally issued driver's license and free outpatient psychiatric care.

The postscript to the physical is that an X-ray showed gallstones which needed to be removed, so we scheduled surgery for Edie. If Edith didn't have bad luck, she wouldn't have any luck at all. Once under the knife, however, the doctor discovered that they weren't really gallstones at all; they were harmless congenital cysts on the gall bladder. While he was already inside, though, he took out her appendix. (What's the insurance reimbursement code for changing procedures in mid-stomach?) The next day, an ashen-faced surgeon visited her room. Edie had been just a few hours away from a ruptured appendix. If he had not removed it, they might well have misdiagnosed the symptoms of a hot appendix as typical post-operative distress. She could have become infected and died! Yo, Rod Serling. Youse want an unbelievable story?

Yo, youse want another? In August we headed back to Georgia and North Carolina for visits with family and friends. In Atlanta, we were to stay in a house across the street from our old neighbors, Shelly and Pete Franklin. In fact, it was his mother's house and she was back in Minnesota for the summer. We got in around mid-afternoon, unpacked, and were ready for cocktail hour when Shelly arrived. Pete wouldn't be joining us, she said, as they had separated! She and her son Brian were living in the house and Pete had taken an apartment in Atlanta. He was out of town all week, but wanted to see us Friday night. Shelly would go out for that evening so Pete could entertain us in their house. (Oooohh, nice heads up on *this* whole situation, Shelly and Pete.) Oh, by the way, says Shelly, none of our mutual friends know about the impending divorce and she'd like us to keep it confidential for now.

We spent the rest of the week lying to our old neighbors.

Friday night we get to hear Pete's rebuttal. (This vacation is turning out to be a *lot* of fun.) So ... Pete gets loaded, has a pots and pans throwing fight with Shelly when she comes home early, and stalks out to his car. Twenty minutes later he is back. He had stopped at a liquor store for replenishment but the clerk said that he was already drunk and refused to sell him any more liquor. Pete went for some bourbon from the home supply. I "persuaded" him that this was not a good idea; he stormed back out before I could grab his keys.

As you might imagine, Edie and I sort of hated to see this blissful evening end, but we trudged across the street for what we hoped would be a peaceful night's sleep. At 2:30 AM, Pete called from a motel near the airport – still drunk – still ranting about Shelly. Then he announced he was going to commit suicide and hung up. Fully awake now, I dialed 911 only to discover that police do not respond to suicide threats, just *actual* suicides. I called the hotel and the night manager promised to check on Pete's room right away. Pete was just drunk, not dead. Meanwhile, Brian was spending the night with us. He was up, of course, asking, "Is that my dad? Doesn't my dad want to talk to me?"

Here's a good traveling lesson: when visiting old neighborhoods, stay in a motel and pre-screen old neighbors. Edie and the kids needed a week at the Jersey shore with Martha when we got home.

Later in the summer, the wall-building Edith had done last year finally caught up with her and a bad back forced her to give up tennis for a while. This respite allowed her to begin a Bible study at church, her first serious reading of God's word, and Edie is enchanted. Speaking of church, Jennifer and Andy were confirmed in November – an important event for all of us. Edie cried though the entire ceremony. Hard. Wonder how it will be at the kids' weddings.

Liz is in 4th grade and goes off to school alone now that Andy is in Junior High. Edie worried about her at first since Andy, her morning mother, leaves early. Who would get her up? Who would make her breakfast? Might, God forbid, her *mother* have to get up early? Well, Edith is simply delighted at how independent Liz has become at nine. So grown up! Good for her.

Andy has forsaken the beetle trap business for steadier employment – a morning paper route. Behind every paperboy stands a nagging mother, a paper-folding mother, a driving-in-the-rain mother. I will ask Andy to split his Christmas tips with Edith.

Jennifer turned 15 last week. Yikes! Are we that old? She is in ninth grade, majoring in swimming and minoring in non-communication. She is <u>very</u> busy, and seemed to be enjoying herself the last time we spoke. Jen has three swim practices a day: 7AM, 3PM, and 7PM. We have a dim candlelight dinner around 5:00 so as not to activate the chlorine in Jen's eyes. In her spare time she talks on the phone. In an emergency you may reach us through our neighbors, the Holtans, at 215-353-2237.

We wish you all a joyous Christmas,

The Cobourns
403 Pine Creek Road
Exton, PA 19341
Christmas, 1980

Merry Christmas,

Ah, another fun-filled year in the lives of the Cobourns. If variety is the spice of life, we're just a big bowl of gumbo.

Edie started the year with another brush with the law – a speeding ticket. Though she had absolutely no chance of winning in court, she chose, of course, to appeal. She was only going five miles over the speed limit, though the cop said fifteen. Besides, a $65 fine equals a car payment. Well, the cop "no-showed." Case dismissed. Edith was bitterly disappointed. She didn't get a chance to tell the judge about the palm trees in Florida being clocked on radar at 30 MPH.

I got a new banjo in the spring. When I was a teenager, I had my mother's old tenor banjo repaired and taught myself to play. But my folk singing idols – Dave Guard of The Kingston Trio and Pete Seeger of The Weavers – played the five-string banjo. I got the name of a banjo maker from a mountain craft store owner in Hendersonville, NC, near my mother's apartment: Homer Ledford from Winchester, Kentucky. Is that an authentic sounding banjo maker, or what? Anyway, this mountain banjo is beautiful, fretted but with no resonator. I had asked Homer to use Grover (threaded) pegs to make it easier to tune, but he installed friction pegs instead. I investigated changing the pegs and took it to the Bucks County Music shop north of Philly. I walked in, plunked my banjo down on the counter and started to ask the proprietor about Grover pegs.

"That's a Ledford, ain't it?" he said.

"How did you know that?" I asked.

"Homer Ledford is one of the best banjo and dulcimer makers in the United States," he replied.

"He's probably made only about 150 banjos."

I knew mine was signed and numbered. "But look here," I said, "Mine is number 497."

> "Hey, if you made banjos, would you number your
> first one '1'?" he asked. "They usually start at two-
> or three-hundred, to make the buyer think he's
> getting a product from an experienced craftsman."

He offered me three times what I had paid for the instrument. I forgot about the pegs and bought a hard-shelled case instead to protect my investment.

I had a little medical jolt this year: a diagnosis of Type II diabetes. I guess I shouldn't have been surprised since my mother is also diabetic. Gotta lose weight and give up Coke and M&M's. Jeez, why don't I just quit drinking and smoking too, while I'm at it? Hey, maybe I'll have a sex change operation and become a cloistered nun!

Andy was a pitcher this year on the Lyonville Youth Association team. One of the advantages of Pennsylvania Little League is our proximity to Williamsport, home of the Little League World Series. During the season, state teams get to play a game in that fabulous stadium. Cabins are available on the grounds for overnights and the kids have a great time. Andy pitched a couple of innings there this summer. When we tell people he played at Williamsport, we sometimes forget to specify that it was not in the World Series. Andy also made honor roll for the fall marking period, so, for his birthday, we upgraded his guitar. We also found him a new guitar teacher who was an instant hit when he asked Andy, "What music do *you* want to learn?" Andy replied, "Air Supply and Heart." Now, what kind of an answer is that? Sounds more like CPR training than guitar lessons.

Meanwhile, Jennifer turns sixteen this month and will soon be driving. Hurrah, we think. At least she can now drive herself to swimming, chorus, swimming, babysitting, swimming, Young Life, and swimming. And Dizzy Lizzy, at 10, is as ornery as ever. Edith is now at the top of her hit list because Edie won't let her join the fifth-grade chorus. Liz is now taking clarinet because band practice is in the afternoon. The chorus practices in the evening, when Jen is probably swimming, and so....well....if you have kids, you probably don't need any further explanation.

This summer, we vacationed for a week with my mother, sister, and brother-in-law Jimmy at Watts Bar resort in Tennessee – a group of rustic cabins and a central dining facility nestled in the shadow of a nuclear reactor. At dinner the first night, Edie ordered the "Catch of the Day."

"What did you catch?" asked the waitress.

"Huh?" answered Edith.

"We clean and cook whatever fish you catch that day."

"Mmmhh," Edith responded.

Oh, great. Now we have to teach Edith how to fish! So Margaret and Edie and I went out early next morning to hunt some bass for dinner. Edie borrowed a pole from Jimmy. After careful instruction from Margaret, the true fisherperson in the family, Edith executed her first cast. Unnerved by the fact that the hook caught the edge of her new floral floppy-brimmed fishing hat, Edith let go of the rod at the end of the cast. With no time for a quick cost analysis, she chose to save her hat. You know, fishing can be boring enough when they're not biting. Edie says when you don't even have a line to put in the water, time barely passes.

I paid Jimmy back for the pole. "Catch of the Day" cost $59.95 that night.

This fall, we lived through our first school strike. Apparently, these happen regularly in Philadelphia. Edie and the kids reversed roles. She resumed her fall activities and the kids stayed home and kept house. This routine was instructive for Jennifer as she becomes a quasi-adult. By the time school finally resumed, she had acquired a discerning eye for housework. My, my, a fastidious teenager. Later in the fall, Jen greeted Edith one afternoon with, "Mom, this place is a mess. You're gonna have to stay home and clean now that I'm back in school."

Hey, who's not a Phillies fan this year? Well, maybe the people in Montreal or Houston. Anyway, I haven't been so excited about baseball since the Braves won two in a row. I had a choice this fall between a playoff game and tickets to "Deathtrap" on Broadway. Guess which Edith made me choose? We took the train up for a matinee and were home before midnight. Actually, the play was a pre-40th birthday present for her since it wasn't at all clear last fall that I would let her live to see 40. Now, just out of spite, I think I will. She's been sending out birthday cards to other 40-year olds for a while now. The last one said, "Do you notice the older you get, the better you feel?" Inside, it said, "Me neither." That just about sums up her attitude on aging.

Halloween was fun again this year. We made Liz up to be a mime (not typecasting). Edie and I went to an adult costume party down the street. Our neighbor, Jim Rowland, and I were the Rock 'n' Roll DJ's. Jim was Pope Rollin' and I was Sister Rockin'. The nun's outfit was just a decoy, though. The party got a little rowdy. By ten, the pope had had more wine than is normal for a Eucharist and started making a move on me. I quickly got out of the habit, revealing underneath my Superman outfit! Order was soon restored and by midnight, after a few puffs of funny smelling smoke, a new Pope was declared.

One of the things that aged Edith this year was her experiment in an investment club. Edith – who can save tin foil, but not money. Not only did she *join* an investment club – she was elected *president*! This is a little like putting Stevie Wonder in charge of your air traffic controllers. The group disbanded at the end of the summer due to lack of interest, but she actually made a profit. I told her she could do anything she wished with the earnings. Our lawnmower died the next weekend. Guess what she wished for?

Finally, my job is still great fun. We celebrated another successful year for the region with a three-day ski trip disguised as a branch managers meeting. The regional staffs are usually the victims at these functions. We're required to develop and present status reports to provide a flimsy justification for the gathering. Rarely do the business sessions last past lunch. In our region, they don't often make it that far. Branch managers at a ski lodge or beachfront resort are not much interested in recruiting statistics, accounts receivable improvements, or time-saving maintenance techniques.

This year, my assistant, Frank Clark, presented our Equal Opportunity accomplishments for 1980 – always a compelling topic. Ten minutes into his pitch, two of the attendees left the room; then another; then a veritable exodus. Soon there were two branch managers left and one was asleep. Frank whispered a frantic aside: "What should I do?" Well, I am a seasoned veteran of such abuse.

"Keep talking. And for God's sake don't let on that you notice anything's wrong." Within a couple of minutes, they started coming back. Each one had a pitcher of beer in his hand.

Now, there are two problems here: First, it's 9:30 in the morning. Second, this behavior is not quite within the spirit of IBM's liquor policy. By now, Frank was terror-stricken. The returning branch managers awakened their sleeping comrade and poured him a cold one. The regional manager left the dais, partly so that Frank would not see him doubled over with laughter, and partly to get a pitcher for himself. Grizzled veteran or not, I knew we were beaten. "Frank," I whispered, "Flip to the last chart and congratulate them on another great year. I'm getting thirsty."

We hope you all had another great year too,

The Cobourns
403 Pine Creek Road
Exton, PA 19341
Christmas, 1981

Happy Holidays,

Must we begin this Christmas letter with yet another story about Edith's little car boo-boos? Hmmm ... yes, we must. It's too good to bury in the middle. Ever since Edie's station wagon body-checked my new Toyota in 1978, I have been renting parking space next door in the Holtan's driveway. Believe me, the monthly rental is far cheaper than body shop and marriage counseling bills. Anyway, with nothing to aim for when leaving the garage, Edith's wagon apparently got confused and left it's rear lid up while backing out. Psychologists call this kind of self-mutilation a plea for attention. The car was lonely. The lid was creased. The garage door was fine.

We put some duct tape on the wagon and packed it up for a weekend in New York City. Edith had long been planning a fun and educational excursion, which Jennifer tried to spoil by making it clear she was *not* looking forward to being away from her swimming buddies for three whole days. Parents of teenagers, however, must not permit themselves to be distracted by their children's opinions. For example, on the way up, Edith democratically asked the kids what they wanted to do in New York.

"See where John Lennon got shot."

"Drive through Harlem."

"Go to the Bowery and look at the bums."

We compromised. We drove quickly by the Dakota, then did all the stuff Edie wanted to do. Luckily, that included a matinee of "Annie."

My aunt and uncle from Chappaqua were our hosts, and my fraternity brother and best man, Dick Ehrlich, and his wife, Susan – both native New Yorkers – were our tour guides. We had an authentic Chinese meal in Chinatown ($26 for the seven of us) and toured Manhattan at night in a way only long-time residents can. Dick showed the kids the Statue of Liberty from a special, secret spot on the tip of the island. We finished with luscious desserts at an obscure little Italian restaurant on 56th. The next day, we had lunch at the Stage Delicatessen and took home an authentic cheesecake ($136 for the five of us). I'll bet that even Jennifer, in the years to come, will remember that trip fondly.

Edie was back on the injured reserve list in tennis this year – BAD sprain warming up at the net before the first match of the spring season. First ambulance ride of her life. First pair of her very own crutches. And her first opportunity to see how her family rallies around when she needs their support.

> Jen: "So *that's* where you were! I tried to call you during second period because I was sick. I was really sick and needed to be picked up."
> Liz: "Well *now* how am I going to get to Girl Scouts?"
> Andy: "I suppose that means you didn't wash my sneaks today."

It was four weeks before she could walk unaided. In the meantime, she rediscovered life's simple pleasures: sunbathing, a Sunday afternoon ride, reading, praying. Lots of time available. God got an earful.

God got an earful from me, too, shortly after I visited Atlantic City this summer. This enlightened community had just installed a casino. Now the mafia doesn't have to travel so far to indulge its depravity. Since New Jersey is part of our territory, several of the less righteous on our regional staff thought we ought to hold a branch managers' meeting there. I had never been to a casino. (Edith doesn't give me any spare money with which to gamble.) So after our afternoon business meeting, I boarded the bus for Resorts International. Maybe if I put a couple of quarters in a slot machine, a waitress bunny would sidle up with a free drink. As I entered the casino, the noise and the glitzy lights smacked me right in the face. Directly in front of me were rows of slots with fat people in bright bowling shirts hunched over them, chain smoking and chain drinking. Beyond were the big gaming rooms, where oily men laid bets the size of my mortgage payment on 22 black.

But another sight seized my attention. Immediately to the left of the front door were the cashiers' windows. One had a long line of the scruffiest individuals I had ever seen. They looked like the vent people in Philadelphia, and they were exchanging their welfare checks for rolls of quarters and silver dollars! They came away from the cages with gleaming eyes, huge smiles displaying all seven or eight teeth, and brows already sweating in anticipation. They headed for the slots. Tonight, for sure, they were going to hit the jackpot and get off welfare. My evening at Resorts suddenly lost much of its charm. I wondered how many kids were shivering at home, waiting for a hot meal. Or whether the taxes paid by those oily men in the other room would be recycled into slot machines next year. I pocketed my quarters and took a cab back to the hotel.

Other than that, my job is still GREAT! I often marvel at how lucky I've been with IBM, particularly when I hear of friends and neighbors who are so desperately unhappy in their careers. As I'm driving to Johnstown or Reading, I sometimes consider what might have been. I remember that IBM fired me in 1963, four months after I was hired. As a sales trainee, I had the technical competence of a slug. After an admirable period of nurturing, the branch manager in Syracuse called me in to trade my ID card for a modest separation check. Surprisingly, the exit interview was interrupted by the administration manager, who announced an opportunity for a supervisory training position in Rochester. The branch manager said if I were willing to pay for the relocation, I could have the job. I quickly exchanged check for card, packed up Edie and all three pieces of furniture, and headed west for Rochester.

And here I am, eighteen years later, in the best job I could imagine. I'm not sure IBM would be quite so patient or gracious today. The irony of the journey from failed sales trainee to regional personnel manager is that it might have been avoided. While packing to move to Philly, I came across the results of a vocational test I took during my junior year in college. It clearly indicated a strength in Human Resources management. Hmmm. Might I have been here sooner by concentrating on those test results? Would I have been as effective without the intervening failures and practical experiences? I'm not so sure.

Early in the summer, Edith and several other mothers took Liz and her scout troop to Chincoteague Island to see the wild horses and giant mutant mosquitoes. As usual, they got more sun than they intended and turned into beets by mid-afternoon. That evening, thanks to the wine brought by one of the better-prepared mothers, the leaders turned into pickled beets. The scouts kept the pickled beets up all night swatting the giant mutant mosquitoes. Edie tells the girls these trips are "learning experiences," a scout leader's euphemism for "dreadful weekends." This is Edith's sixth year as a Girl Scout leader. She *finally* knows what she's doing, just as Liz is talking about quitting! Edie has buzzard's luck: Can't find nothin' to kill; can't find nothin' that's already dead.

Liz had another interesting learning experience this summer. Edie took the kids to the shore again to visit Martha for a week. (Don't ever tell Edith that I enjoy their vacations as much as they do. The peace and quiet of a house devoid of teenagers is an awesome and mystical experience.) Anyway, we have a snapshot of Liz feeding seagulls while simultaneously ducking seagull poop. Wouldn't you think that by eleven she'd recognize the connection? Don't the Girl Scouts teach you that stuff?

Although this summer was brief, due to last fall's school strike, we did manage to get all the kids off to camp in August. Jen went to a Young Life camp in Colorado – a fifty-hour bus ride for a mountaintop experience – but Jen and her friends loved every minute of it; and the rappelling, rafting, singing, and mountain climbing weren't bad either.

Liz wanted to go to a horse camp but, since such a venture is typically followed by irrational pleas for a horse, we compromised and sent her to a local Girl Scout camp. Her letters home attested to the wonderful time she had:

> "This food is terrible! Please send me some candy.
> Shana and Marcy are still fighting. Don't forget the
> candy. I threw up Wednesday, but I'm OK now. I
> need candy, PLEASE!!!"

Andy resisted the idea of camp at first, but relented when Edith found him a co-ed teen high-adventure Y camp at Lake Placid. Andy backpacked through snow, rain, and threats of bears and loved every co-ed minute of it. We stayed home and luxuriated in the quiet. We took gourmet picnics to the banks of the Brandywine and talked about how many days were left before we had to pick up the kids.

Now the cold Pennsylvania winter is upon us. Because our builder, Ray Charles, got a great deal on heat pumps, that's what we all have here in Pine Creek Valley, despite the fact that they're ineffective much farther north than Richmond. So we're chopping wood and stocking up on kerosene to avoid $400 a month heating bills. Our next-door neighbor can't wait for menopause so at least the hot flashes will keep her warm.

We hope you're warm this Christmas, and that you have a happy New Year,

The Cobourns
110 Canter Court
Roswell, GA 30076
Christmas, 1982
(Dated 2/7/83)

Merry Christmas everyone!!

Er, Happy Epiphany!!!

Of course we didn't forget you. Nor did we cross you off our Christmas list. We know how important our letter is to your mental health for the coming year. Only by wading through our year with us, can you sit back, look at your year objectively, and realize what a splendid one it was by comparison.

One reason we're late in writing is that Edith and I hit an all-time high in volunteerism this fall. We signed on as Fruit Chairmen for the high school chorus. The Roswell High band and chorus hold a big November fund-raiser peddling boxes of fruit to unsuspecting parents and neighbors. It was pure stupidity on my part to chair an event we had never attended, much less worked on. But with two kids in chorus, I felt we must do something to help, and this $4,000 money-raiser looked like a one-shot deal. More than 300 person-hours later, on December 16, the fruit arrived – LATE! Some 1400 boxes of oranges, tangelos and grapefruit that required unloading, sorting, mixing, and delivering. Well, we're still alive to tell the tale, and we made $5,000. We were so proud of the kids, and were about to tell them so, when the choral director said he'd hoped we'd do better! We forgive him for not understanding that 125 percent of quota *is* fundamental goodness. Anyway, as we turned in our sixteen-page notebook entitled, "How To Avoid the Pitfalls of Citrus '82," I told Edith that, with this experience, we should chair the sale next fall and, this time, really do it right. To which Edith replied, "(Expletive deleted.)"

As many of you know, we are back in Georgia again. For those of you who want to grow up to be a corporate gypsy like me, here are some cautions while preparing your family for a move:

1. Do not assume, just because your family was sad to leave Atlanta four years ago, that they are yearning to return now.
2. Do not expect teenaged children to experience the thrill of *your* promotion. They could not care less if *you* were banished to the Gulag, as long as *they* are not separated from their friends.
3. The promise of season tickets to the Atlanta Braves is not a compelling argument for your wife to relocate.

Our star led us back to Roswell, where we found the perfect house. To me that means one with only twenty minutes' worth of grass to mow. We are on the other side of town from our old neighborhood – different schools and recreation facilities – in a very real sense, a whole fresh start. We might as well have gone to Kansas City.

We bought the house from an extraordinarily fastidious (read "childless") couple. He traveled all week and she locked herself in the house, frightened of any outside contact. Every door and window was equipped with deadbolts. The windows had never been opened. She ran either the heat or A/C year round! She kept the floodlights on at night and had alarm company stickers on all the windows. When we moved in, I discovered a loaded .38 special she kept in the closet just in case a band of gypsies invaded the neighborhood. My neighbor said this woman was so obsessively cleanly that she made her husband go outside to change his mind. Well, the house *was* immaculate – then the kids unpacked.

We got back to Georgia just in time to see the Gardner Holden Randall, Sr. family relocate to Houston. So much for stable communities and life-long neighbors. The IBM's and Xerox's of the world have ensured that, if *you* don't move, your neighbor will. We are getting very good at giving and receiving going-away parties: hugs and promises to write/visit/call often; Rhett and Scarlett T-shirts, dogwood cross-stitches, azalea watercolors, and magnolia centerpieces. All teary reminders of life as you wish it could have remained. Memories quickly thrust aside as you once again begin the search for a new doctor, dentist, mechanic, bank, church, swim team, tennis club and, one hopes, a friend or two.

Re-entering a town where you once lived, though, has its funny moments. One of the first neighbors Edith met turned out to be a Kappa. You can spot Kappas easily because they use fleur-de-lis note pads and carry hand towels with little blue owls all over them. The neighbor insisted on taking Edith to the Kappa meeting that week. Edie tried to prepare herself for it, since no one in the group knew we had moved back. She thought of the commotion she would cause – lots of embraces, maybe a few squeals of "EDITH!!!! What are you doing back?"

Guess what? Two people (out of forty) remembered her, and *they* arrived late. To the rest, she was just a vaguely familiar face they hadn't seen in a while.

As if the anonymity wasn't bad enough, the program that day was on Color Analysis – a new-wave religion based on salvation through wearing the "proper" colors. As they decided whether they were Springs or Autumns, Edith knew not where her identity lay. I told her I thought she might be a Thursday. But I understood her mood that night as she related her story. Someone in the elevator at work that morning had said to me, "Hey, Tom! I haven't seen you in a long time! Are you over in Building 7?"

"No, we just moved back; we've been gone since 1978."

"Oooohhhh. That's right. You went to Chicago. Welcome back."

Yes, it's a thrill to make lasting impressions.

The Gardner Holden Randall, Srs. didn't move the very day after we returned, though. We had time for one more adventure. This time, Honee, Mrs. Gardner Holden Randall, Sr. , had won a weekend at a condo on Tybee Island off Georgia's coast – you know, one of those deals where you agree to let Willie Loman try to sell you a timeshare in exchange for a "free" two-day stay? So Gardner Holden Randall, Sr. rented a plane to fly us down. (Hadn't I told you that in between rugby matches he had gotten his pilot's license?)

As we dodged the hailstones on the way to the Peachtree-Dekalb airport, several of us suggested to the captain that we scrap the weekend and order in a pizza instead. Such signs of cowardice

44

tend to infuriate Gardner Holden Randall, Sr., prompting him to drive faster so we can taxi out before the storm subsides. Luckily, we got there in time to take off in the rain. God was sending His clearest signs that this trip was not a part of His master plan for us, but our flight schedule was the Gospel according to Gardner, who buzzed Stone Mountain on the way to the coast. We don't think he meant to, but he took credit for it anyway. An eternity later, we landed in Savannah: Luke Skywalker and three sissies. Willie Loman's sales pitch didn't seem so bad after all.

Our biggest news this year – with all deference to A. A. Milne – is "Now We Are Six." Martha, Edith's sister, is with us. After a couple of bouts with job layoffs in the NYC/NJ area over the last few years, we convinced her to come south where we knew the job market was better. She arrived at the end of August, when the "Fall Busies" were upon us: soccer and chorus and swimming and sleep-overs and The Rocky Horror Picture Show. She saw us spending 20 minutes each night determining how two cars and four drivers could get six people wherever they needed to be. Her comment: "You have made 'One Flew Over the Cuckoo's Nest' a reality for me." Martha is matting and framing for an art gallery here while deciding whether Atlanta is where she wants to be.

Now ... the kids. Liz at age 12 is working hard in 7th grade on report writing – getting lots of encouragement (prodding) from her Aunt Martha. In the four seasons we've been here, Liz has participated in two old sports, softball and swimming, and two new sports, cheerleading and basketball. Three cheers for Liz in this "Age of the Specialized Child." Her first friend in the neighborhood introduced her to cheerleading and, from that moment on, all we heard was, "*Please*, can't I cheer for the 67 lb. football team?" (In this age group, the cheerleaders often weigh more that the players.)

At the risk of offending all you former "Rahs," cheerleading was not high on Edith's list. With lots of nudging from 18-year old Jennifer, who was once 12, Edith finally said, "Yes, if you agree to swim this summer for the Roswell Rec. team." Edie clearly did not focus on the fact that swim practice would start every morning at 7:30 AM. Liz was home by 9 saying, "*Now* what do I do for the rest of the day?"

And Edie's luck didn't get any better with cheerleading. The team mother, who had never let out a crotch in her life, picked a skirt pattern with godets (which is French for "hard to make") and a plaid material. Thank God for Martha or the outfit would still be on the cutting board. By the way, did you know there is a "gift for cheerleading?" Well, there is, and Liz has it. As for the "gift for basketball", we're not sure yet. In the first game she played, she shot at the wrong basket. Luckily, she missed. Four games later, she got to play again and scored four points for her team in a 22-8 victory.

If you're looking for Andy these days, he's at the refrigerator – trying to find enough food to make him be 6' 10". He's 15 and growing like Georgia kudzu. His former growth rate could be likened to that of a magnolia tree. He thinks growing tall is wonderful, but it tears us up to give away jeans whose knees are still dark blue. In December, Andy tried out for the All-State Chorus and made first cuts, an accomplishment that not even he expected given that, depending on whether he had had chili the night before, he could sing either baritone or tenor. He's waiting to hear whether he made final cuts. Andy is wearing contacts now. We hope his eyes don't grow. Next to contacts, Andy's most frequent request was to upgrade his electric guitar (to one that works). This, too, came to pass last fall when he cashed in some of his coin collection. Apparently, the fundamental concept of an electric guitar is to play it at the pain threshold. Whatever happened to 'soft' rock?

Andy has been employed briefly as a busboy at a local restaurant. The fact that he was hired despite the Georgia State Child Labor laws is of no consequence since, before he "retired," he had earned enough for a plane ticket to Philadelphia. He and Jen returned to Philly the week after Christmas and both had a blast thanks to our dear friends and former neighbors, the Holtans, who provided them room and board. Did Andy stand at your refrigerator, Paul? We owe you $87.50.

Jennifer: Never move a Senior in high school. Edie thought it was bad enough when her parents moved her as a Junior. Well, finally dear sweet Jen is again speaking to us. More importantly, as a friend pointed out, she is still taking our money. That is a key signal in your relationship with your teenager. She is trying hard to be a part of Roswell High while her heart is still in Philadelphia. She misses her good buddy, Gwen. And Randy, and Michael, and.......so much so that she mowed lawns and lifeguarded last summer so she could fly back to see them. We had the lawn mower engine rebuilt while she was gone. I think we should have just bought the ticket.

Jen also took up sewing to keep busy last summer. Typical teenage immediate gratification: sew it today – wear it tonight! Eight non-stop hours later it was finished. Jen tried it on and immediately realized she'd bought the wrong size pattern.

"@#$%^*&&%@@," she said.

With puppy-dog eyes, she asked Edith to re-do it. The sewing project, designed to keep Jen busy, took her one day and Edie three. Ha!

After gathering all kinds of tips on the college search for Jen, we decided in November to move to Plan B: Apply Somewhere Quick! She has been accepted at Auburn and the University of Georgia (how 'bout them dawgs!), and is waiting to hear from James Madison. I think she'll be glad when this is all settled. In the meantime, keep swimming, Jen. Get a scholarship and we'll let you go wherever you want.

The biggest thing that happened to me in 1982 was having my toenails removed – an event caused by a fungus under my two big toenails. Yuucccchhhhh!!! The kids had a real good time with, "There's a fungus amungus." But, three days post-op, I was in church, dressed in my blue pin stripes and sandals and bandaged toes. I told the minister that this is how Jesus would have looked if He had worked for IBM.

The next highlight of the year was my debut with Jennifer in the Roswell Women's Club Revue. Jen and I sang Paul Stookey's "The Wedding Song" with me accompanying on the banjo. I can't tell you how nervous Edith was. What if we messed up in front of all those people? Could she just deny she knew us? Luckily, there were enough worse acts that we sounded pretty good ... and she could be proud.

I must tell you about Cobourn's Rainbow – the last story – I promise. We were trying so hard in August to convince Martha to come to Atlanta. As you can imagine, she was having a real struggle deciding to leave New Jersey after 23 years. We were praying for God's guidance and feeling very inadequate. On August 9th (Edie recorded it on her calendar) Andy spotted a rainbow touching down in our back yard – right off the deck. So close, you could almost grab it. We ran outside to see where it ended....couldn't believe our eyes....right in our front yard! Our own personal rainbow from God, saying "I am with you." It lasted only a few minutes, but it will be with us forever. We are still awestruck by the thought. It is hard to write about miracles, but on that note, we wish you all

God's best for 1983,

The Cobourns
110 Canter Court
Roswell, GA 30076
Christmas, 1983

Christmas greetings once again,

1983! What an incredible year of challenges, trials, solutions and rewards. I hardly know where to begin. But that's never stopped me before.

Ever heard the expression, "Lean upon the Lord?" Edith didn't lean this year. She sat on His lap and wrapped her arms around His neck.

When we last left our continuing saga, her sister, Martha, was with us. Remember? Sisters together again after 23 years? Each coming at life from a totally different direction? By spring, it was clear that what Martha wanted most was to be independent again. She had become increasingly depressed. Though we encouraged her to get some counseling, she resisted. Finally, after Edie and I agonized for several days, we insisted that Martha get help or move out. You can imagine the pain for Edith, risking the alienation of her only sister. Martha, of course, was devastated. Having been persuaded last year to leave an awful situation in New Jersey, now she found the Atlanta solution was not at all what she had hoped.

The immediate logistical problem was wheels. Martha had been saving and looking for a car without much luck until, on May 16, we were given a car, a 1970 Buick Skylark, by our church. It was in "good" running condition, but I had seen better looking cars abandoned along New York's Hutchison River Parkway. Well, within a week, Martha had moved in with some friends and, to date, is still working at an art gallery framing shop.

The guest bedroom was empty all summer. For a couple of weeks, we enjoyed visiting friends in Philly, Rochester, and Syracuse. The occasion was my 25th High School Reunion in July. There is some solace in being together with 100 others in varying stages of fatness, baldness and wrinkledness. Then they give you a name tag with your high school picture on it to remind you, dramatically, that you are from an era when "Happy Days" was a reality.

Anyway, the trip was great fun and our little Toyota, heavily laden, groaned through all 2,000 miles; a tad cramped with four people, but superb gas mileage. Yes, this was our first vacation without Jennifer, and we missed her. She had to work so she could afford all the parties at the University of Georgia this fall.

While Jen spent 60+ hours a week at her job, Edith spent August getting her ready for college. Parting of mother and child was DIFFICULT! Edie thought her heart would break, but she overcame the grief with support from family and friends. I was a big comfort, of course. My wise counsel included such insights as "The Lord never gives you a burden greater than you can bear." Edith wished He didn't think so highly of her.

But new "opportunity" forced Edith to accelerate the transition. My mom came to live with us for a while. At 72, she decided the time had come to give up her apartment, a decision made urgent because of several falls – the result, we think, of small strokes. She had stoically accepted the idea of a retirement home and finally agreed on a lovely place called Budd Terrace in Atlanta. The period from decision to move-in, however, was not without trauma. There was a three month waiting period, during which time she had a couple of bouts in the hospital, one after a stomach virus dropped her sodium count so low she had a slight seizure. Then, after three weeks in a nursing home, with physical therapy to regain her strength, she moved to Budd Terrace on December 6. We are delighted to report she is back to her old self: chipper, witty, and walking better than ever. She says she really loves the place and we are thrilled she's so close.

Now then, two memorable and hysterical moments to add to our scrapbook – the first giving further evidence of Edith's faultless judgment and timing. It began during a traffic jam on the way to Disney World in February. We were spending four days there with the Matthaidesses. The first three days were crummy and rainy and cold. You wouldn't wish such weather on your worst enemy (well, maybe your *really* worst enemy). But did we let that dampen our spirits? Never! Anyway, the lines were short. The fourth day the sun came out. And so did the crowds. Thus, the traffic jam. Our top speed was one mile per hour and it looked like we might not get into the park until next Thursday.

Our stomachs were grumbling and so were we. Then, 1,000 yards ahead, Edith spotted those famous Golden Arches. Brainstorm! She took breakfast orders and she and the kids trotted ahead to McDonalds. Just as they picked up the order, the traffic started to move faster ... then a little faster ... then a lot faster. So there they were, four kids, $30 worth of Egg McMuffins, and an old broad racing down a median strip, trying to catch their car. I thought she'd have a heart attack, but she just got real sweaty real early.

The second notable moment came while the Rowlands were visiting from Philadelphia during a typical Atlanta August: HOT. We decided a raft ride down the Chattahoochee would cool us off, so we picked a relatively uninhabited section of the river for a quiet, peaceful trip. We now know why that section of the river is relatively uninhabited. Because it is relatively unnavigable. Observed by several super-sophisticated, Coors-chugging teenagers lounging on the rocks, we entered the water with style and grace. We ran aground three feet later. It was clear that our beer chests needed a deeper draft. So we pushed and dragged and slipped our way to deeper water and finally got underway. Boy, if Tom Sawyer had had that much trouble, Mark Twain would be running a lingerie boutique in Joplin, Missouri.

Now for the kids: Liz is an eighth grader at a new middle school in Roswell. She has decided to become a good student and demonstrate acceptable behavior in school this year. Tears blurred Edith's vision at the fall conference as she listened to all the teachers sing praises of Liz. ("Liz who?," I said, turning around, "You mean Liz Abbott over on Saddle Horn Circle?") Edie told Liz she was a great example of repentance – reminding her of a Sunday School discussion we'd had recently. "I am?" she asked. "Then can I get some more nail polish tomorrow?"

Liz's dreams came true when she attended Camp Skyline in Alabama last summer, visited her old friends in Philly, and when she finally got to see The Nutcracker last week. Cheerleading still ranks high on her list of priorities. The cheerleaders' dress pattern was easier this year (or it would have been if Edie hadn't put all that white piping in the wrong places). Liz also plays on the neighborhood tennis team and is anxious to volunteer as a Candystriper this fall at a new area hospital.

Andy seems to be working harder for grades this year, too. We caught him doing homework one night in October. Literally took our breath away. His incentive? College applications next year. In the meantime, when he's not studying, he's singing with the Roswell High Chorus, or as a member of their newly formed male quartet, or alone accompanied by one of his guitars. With Jen gone, he misses his downstairs cleaning companion. We know now who did most of the cleaning, so Edith had to give him her crash course in bathroom sanitation. If only she had done this sooner, we wouldn't have had all those little worms curled up in the corners. Oh, well …

Andy also plays a lot of tennis – on both the high school and Saddle Creek teams – but his biggest sports challenge this year was coaching a children's soccer team. He was not told that the boys were four years old. He discovered quickly that not only did they not know their left foot from their right, but they didn't particularly care which goal they shot at. Sometimes, at a critical moment, they just stood at midfield and cried. He loved the little kids, but concluded that four year-olds should not play competitive sports.

The highlight of Andy's year was a week at Ridgecrest, a Baptist Conference Center in the North Carolina mountains. Invited to go by a friend, it turned out to be a wonderful experience for him. He's OK about his new-found faith and spends much of his time with three active youth groups in town: Episcopal, Baptist and Fellowship Bible. How's that for ecumenism? He is looking forward to another week at Ridgecrest and a ski trip in January with the Fellowship Youth Group.

Jennifer has just completed her first quarter at the University of Georgia in Athens. She is a Pi Phi pledge and lives in an all girls dorm, which she loves. She also loves having her best buddy, Gwen (from Philly), at Georgia with her. When asked how she likes college, she will tell you, "It's OK." By that she means the classes are hard, she hasn't decided on a major, the social pressures are immense, and she's not sure what she's going to do when she grows up. She also misses her family. After seven years of competitive swimming, she finally retired this summer to coach a swim team at a nearby club. She even hired an assistant coach, Mark, a fellow Roswell High graduate who is in his first year at Clemson. By mid-summer, I had seen Mark at the house often enough to realize that this was not the standard employer-employee relationship. He is now, with Gwen and Jen, one of our three favorite college kids.

Jen just celebrated her 19th birthday. That means she's "legal" in Georgia. Her most frequent question lately is, "Dad, are you sure you don't need anything at the liquor store?" For her birthday, we let her get two moles removed and have all her wisdom teeth out. She looked like a chipmunk, but her complexion is flawless. Mostly, she enjoyed the anesthetic. In the recovery room, her mouth stuffed with gauze, she wrote Edie a note saying, "I feel great! I'm coming here more often. Can I get some anesthetic to go?" We hope her face is fine by the time she flies to Philly for an after-Christmas visit.

I am in my third job since moving back to Roswell. Andy thinks IBM is trying to tell me something. I'm currently manager of the department responsible for employment, placement, and personnel strategy for the National Marketing Division. However, Edith's nagging and the limited amount of attention the kids pay to my requests keep me humble. Edie nagged me back into tennis last spring. I joined a newly formed men's team in Saddle Creek. We won three points (not matches – points) all season. We looked like the Helen Keller Memorial Tennis Team. Luckily, we improved in the fall.

Edie and I played on a mixed doubles team this summer – a test of marriage comparable only to participating in a weekly bridge club or hanging wallpaper. I also tried my hand at deck gardening in June. We grew little tomatoes in big pots. They were root-bound within a week. They tasted good but looked like cherry tomatoes with under-active thyroids. I am still layreading at church and singing in the choir. We have also volunteered the Von Cobourn Family Singers for the early Christmas service again this year.

One advantage to moving so much is that you can do the same music year after year (until your boy soprano becomes a baritone).

As for Edith, I think she's found her niche in Christian Education. She has been part of a marvelous Bible Study on James this fall. In January, our parish is beginning "Bethel," a two-year overview of the Bible. Ten folks volunteered to take the course, and at the end of the two years they will be prepared to teach it to the rest of the congregation. Edie continues to teach sixth, seventh, and eighth Grade Sunday School – an ever-humbling experience. Several weeks ago, after working very hard on the lesson, she was tremendously excited about the insight she expected the kids to get from her work. Too late, she realized that she had not given the same attention to the opening prayer. As she stumbled through what was probably her most forgettable petition, one of the 12 year-olds nudged her and said, "You just made that up, didn't you."

I helped answer another of her prayers in November when I treated her to five days in San Francisco. What a great trip! In addition to the city, we toured the Napa Valley and spent a day in Monterey and Carmel. But the best part for Edie was five days with no responsibilities.

Finally, we had a wonderful Thanksgiving with the Matthaidesses. They came down to visit their son, Dave, who is stationed at Fort Gordon. We all had a great reunion, which included a trip to the Ebenezer Baptist Church (Martin Luther King's) in Atlanta.

We are thankful for our dear friends and relatives and wish you all God's best in 1984,

The Cobourns
110 Canter Court
Roswell, GA 30076
Christmas, 1984

Christmas Cheer,

I have a new toy – this computer. Edith says I never talk to her anymore. She says she would rather compete with another woman. Her jealousy is unfounded. I have named my computer "Bruce." As you will see later, Bruce can also do compound sentences. Anyway, for those of you already offended by typewritten Christmas letters, I know this must be even harder to bear. Take heart. Edith has convinced me not to address them to "Occupant."

Edie characterizes 1984 in two words: "MENTALLY EXHAUST-ING." As a traffic cop for three teenagers (oops, Jen is 20) going in three different directions, she finds life complicated. "Stand your ground!" she exhorts herself. "Be firm! Hold onto what you know is right!" After protecting our kids from the evils of the world, she falls into bed at night absolutely drained. Does she understand mid-life crisis? You betcha.

Just weeding out good trends from bad is a challenge. I can't think of one 1984 trend that wins our whole-hearted support – certainly not the baggy look. I believe we're all baggy enough already. Nor do we approve of high school Juniors and Seniors driv-ing to school every day when they could ride the bus. (That's why God made school buses.) Traffic jams, which are worse now in the suburbs than in the city, are maddening. And, while I'm at it, I don't like our new "Super Kroger" which requires a twenty-five minute hike before you even get to the groceries! Now you can get oil filters, videos, prescriptions, an abortion, and a new set of tires to go along with your produce.

And school shopping this fall blew us away. We now have preppy, beachwear, new wave.....a whole department for each look. Who needs it? Remember when all the sweaters were in one section instead of spread out among 12 different labels? Edie told the girls that when she was their age, department stores had sportswear, lingerie, and shoes. That was it! They all wore plaid pleated skirts – whether they looked good in them or not – and the only difference in sweaters was whether your parents could afford cashmere or orlon.

Whew! We feel better already having gotten all that off our chests. Edie feels so good now she's considering taking up cooking again. Her cooking in '84 slipped to an all-time low....probably the result of mental exhaustion (see above). We went from having pizza only as a special treat to calling Domino's periodically and telling them *not* to deliver tonight.

Well, after 30 YEARS, I quit smoking on Ash Wednesday (inadvertent pun). THREE PACKS A DAY! COLD TURKEY! Edith quit in 1971 and my father died of emphysema in 1974. She is surprised it took me this long, but offers a "Hallelujah. Praise the Lord!"

A year ago, IBM asked me to revise its smoking policy, moving toward greater consideration for non-smokers. It soon became clear from my research that all business offices would eventually become no-smoking facilities, so I used Lent as a prompt to quit. Incredibly, God immediately visited upon me the WORST respiratory something-or-other I have ever had! For four days, I couldn't smell or taste, caught only shallow breaths, and I *certainly* couldn't smoke. That took care of the hardest period of withdrawal. I'm convinced that God helped me "pick my time." It doesn't justify my not having quit earlier, but these are complex and emotional addictions. Walk up to an alcoholic and tell him that, starting tomorrow, you'd like him never to drink again. See how effective *that* strategy is

1984 was the year we got our fair share of IBM's medical benefits. Liz started out by having her tonsils removed in March. Poor kid. For four days she just motioned or rang her bell. Then, for the next three days, she sounded like a 78 record played at 33 1/3. Next, she got braces. Edie got bifocals so she could see the braces. Now Edie's tennis shoes appear larger when she looks down and she whiffs on the serve when she looks up. November was my big medical month. First, a kidney stone (may you never have to pass a kidney stone); then, the total removal of a toenail (may you never have a big toe that looks like a hammerhead shark). I'm fully recovered now, but I do tilt a little to the right.

Whew! medical bills, college bills, nursing home bills; anyone else out there heard this story before? We soon received a notice from American Express telling us our spending and payment patterns had qualified us for the Lead level card, and our new limit was $137.24. We had just enough cash left to get new floor mats for the car. By the way, do you remember when all cars had rubber flooring? Well, do you remember your parents telling you about it? Then somebody decided that auto buyers wanted the luxury of carpet. And then, so as not to get the carpet dirty, they sold us rubber floor mats. Now, we have carpeted rubber floor mats. Think about it.

Those floor mats were for my new car in which, for the first month, kids were not allowed to eat anything which could crumble or soil. During the second month, we drove it to Houston to spend a week with the Gardner Holden Randall, Srs. Andy, newly licensed, put a minor dent in the hood in that horrible Houston traffic. On the way home, we blew a tire on I-10. Once safely home, Andy put a major dent in the hood in that horrible Atlanta traffic. My new cars don't stay new too long. Jen and Edith were just glad that, for a change, they hadn't done the damage.

Liz, our baby at 14, had her long hair reduced to a short bob in preparation for her freshman year of high school. Her year has included confirmation, swimming and piano lessons, a great week at Clemson tennis camp, and a vacation at Hilton Head with Mom, Dad, and her best buddy Erin. This fall, Liz went to her first college fraternity party. ("You mean Jen," people say when I tell this story.) No, Liz! Jennifer graciously invited us all up to Athens for Homecoming. Edie and I stayed in a motel. Andy bunked with a friend from Roswell. Jen asked Liz to stay in her dorm room. Well, that night, Andy, Jen, and her roommate decided to check out the Kappa Sig party..... What were they going to do? Leave Liz alone in the dorm? Heaven forbid! Andy assured me the next morning that the party was fine – just a band playing. I had to laugh, though, when I picked Liz up from school the next Monday. She slammed the car door and said,

"Man, I can't wait to get out of this place."

"What place?" I said.

"High school," said Liz. "I want to go to college!"

Andy, 17 and a high school senior, is preoccupied with college applications. He has been accepted at UGA, but will reserve his decision until he hears from Furman and Sewanee. I'm hoping for Georgia.....think it would great to have two kids going in the same direction again. Andy's favorite outfit is high-top sneakers, baggy pants, and one of my old T-shirts with the sleeves cut off. Fetching! The last item we consider inappropriate school wear, so Edie has to check under his Army jacket each morning to see that he has a real shirt on. His favorite pastimes include anything to do with music, especially playing the guitar or going to a good concert (e. g. INXS, Frankie Goes To Hollywood, The Psychedelic Furs, or REM). What ever happened to names like "The Four Lads?"

Andy still sings with the Varsity Chorus and was selected for the Georgia All-State Chorus again. His most memorable musical moment this year, for me anyway, was his accompanying our duet in a church folk mass. We did a great song called "Jesus Walkin' on the Water." It's just as well that our very proper Anglican choir director will never know that Andy got the song from a Violent Femmes album!

We rang in Jen's 20th birthday with a surprise party. Our first time to entertain the college crowd. Edie was a bit nervous. Jen, as a sophomore, has gone from strongly disliking UGA and what it has to offer, to loving it. Pi Phi has played a big part in this transition. She served this year as assistant pledge trainer, and she loves singing in their Washboard Band. Lest she should ever have an idle moment, she joined the Pi Sigma Epsilon business fraternity. Her pledge project: the Baxter Street Blitz, a progressive pub party which raised $1500 and earned her team the award for Outstanding Marketing Project. She's in pre-journalism, but still has no clue as to a major. This summer she coached swimming, gave lessons, and was an assistant pool manager – lots of pressure, but she learned a lot and enjoyed it. Jen says her love life is "slim to none" (which is OK by me).

We see my mom at least a weekly now that she's an Atlanta resident and only 40 minutes away. She suffered another slight stroke in October, which landed her in the rehab section of Wesley

Woods for physical therapy. She has made marvelous progress, though. She is walking a little again and she hasn't lost her sense of humor. As she and a friend say, "At least we're OK from the waist up!" Her most recent outing was a trip to our house for Christmas day – a treat for both her and us.

As for Edith, she read one book this year. Actually, part of one book – the Old Testament – in her Bethel Bible Study teacher training class. Ten hours of homework each week and a four-hour final exam which turned out to be one essay question: "Write the history of the nation of Israel." This month, they begin the New Testament, and next fall, they start teaching the course. This prospect scares her, but I guess she'll be alright teaching biblically illiterate Episcopalians. This course, by the way, has solved her Trivial Pursuit-esteem deficit. She now asks me Baby Boomer questions and I ask her Bible Trivia. She already has three wedges.

Her most difficult job this year was captain of her tennis team. Despite her new-found biblical wisdom, she could not keep fourteen unpaid women happy. It's not easy to tell Janice that, although her finger sandwiches are as good as ever, her backhand is slipping and she no longer moves well to her right. Janice, of course, believes she'd be playing #1 – if only she weren't cursed with Marilyn as her partner.

Since I started on such a negative note, I must end on a positive one: Edie's 1985 tip for making Enforced Family Outings with three teenagers bearable. Enforced Family Outings (EFO's) are desperate measures parents take to preserve the illusion that teenagers are still considered part of the family. ("But mom, I don't want to visit the Johnsons with you. They're so creepy.") EFO's fall into the category of parental nurturing characterized by the explanation: "BECAUSE I SAY SO, THAT'S WHY!!!" The key to success is Advanced Notice.

If you want to attend the Robert Shaw Christmas Concert in December, tell them in September. When they're reminded the week of the concert, you may get an evil glare, but they really have no excuse. ("I *told* you about this in September.") It also helps to plan outings during their "off hours." Three to five PM is good because they're out of bed and their evening activities have not yet begun. This worked out for our "Family Trim-A-Tree" party this year. Everyone showed up – clean and acceptably attired – and it brought tears to our eyes.

Well, Bruce, you did a pretty good job. Miraculous, these computers.

We wish you miracles, too, for 1985,

The Cobourns
110 Canter Court
Roswell, GA 30076
Christmas, 1985

Merry Christmas,

Ah, the Holidays are here again. For us, that means two-thirds of our kids come home. At Thanksgiving, the arrival of Andy, now a freshman at the University of Georgia, was followed closely by the arrival of a couple of his high school friends – Dave and Peter – freshmen at Georgia Tech and Wake Forest, respectively. We overheard their newly acquired insight on intellectual growth in general and college studies in particular:

> Dave: You know, I think my parents like me better now that I'm at college.
> Andy: Probably because you're not home so often.
> Dave: Yeah, maybe. At Georgia Tech, they tell us we're "designing tomorrow today!" But I haven't really learned anything yet.
> Peter: Boy, I have! In ROTC, I learned what to pack when going on a desert raid.
> Dave: Well, really, I guess I have learned how much air pressure one molecule of air exerts on a wall.
> Andy: Oh, *that's* useful.
> Dave: Yeah, like the other night at dinner my mom was saying, "Gee, I wonder how much pressure that air molecule over there is exerting on the dining room wall?"
> Andy: I know. That's why I'm so glad I'm taking Anthropology. Just last week my dad asked me, "Andy, is that BaMbuti tribe in Central Africa as egalitarian a society as they say?"

And so on. I hope Dave's parents feel as rewarded as we do about the thousands of dollars they are shelling out. And then, because we're on the University of Georgia mailing list, we get these frequent pleas from some post office box in New Jersey:

"Send your student a CARE PACKAGE for exam week!!! INCLUDES REESE'S PIECES, GRANOLA BARS, AND A CANDLE WITH WICKS ON BOTH ENDS. And it will mean SO MUCH to him/her, because he/she knows it's from YOU/YOU!!! (Only $9.95 per quarter. ACT NOW!!)"

Some guy in Ridgewood, NJ, has just sent his whole family to Princeton on our collective $9.95's. I throw out all the mail addressed to: CAR-RTE-SORT 30076 ......

At any rate, the dialogue above is significantly more uplifting than most of the conversations between Elizabeth and her friends:

Liz: And so I was like, "WOW!"

Friend: Yeah? So then he goes, "And she was like, 'Really!?'"

Liz: Well, what did you say?

Friend: Well, you know, I go, like, "Hey!"

Jen also came home for Thanksgiving. Actually, she left the motor running while she dropped off her laundry and picked up the video club card before driving to the mall with Carolyn. We did sort of catch up on her life, though, as she backed out the door: "If LeeAnne calls, tell her I'll call her back. If Vickie or Lisa calls, take a message. And, Dad, if Fred calls, don't make any jokes!!!! PLEASE!!!! ...."

Jen is the Social Chairman of Pi Phi this year. She lives at the house in a room they call "THE ZOO," not because the cook throws raw meat in there every morning (How 'bout them dawgs), but because there are two other officers in the room and there is always a meeting going on. I asked Jen what she needed for Christmas and she said, "Sleep!"

Liz got her driver's permit this fall. My insurance man followed her home from the license bureau with some suggestions as to how I might help him afford his new boat. Liz will be our third to TURN SIXTEEN, and I don't know if my pacemaker can be turned up another notch. Now she has her braces off, and her permit, and pink high-top sneakers, and contact lenses, and so much mascara that her head droops forward a little – proving once again, gentle reader, that there is no peaceful transition from childhood to adulthood. It happens while you are at work one day. You come home and say,

"Edie, where's Liz? Oh, you *are* Liz!" As was true with us all, with maturity comes poverty. Just when they are responsible enough to babysit, they don't want to babysit anymore. They want to go out. But how can they afford to go out if they don't babysit?

Edith is as busy as ever. She finished her two-year Bethel Bible Study teachers' class this spring. Liz and I thought that we would now be fed on Wednesday nights, but Edie was one of the first two chosen to teach Bethel. She earned it! So, we still fix our own hamburgers on Wednesdays. As in,

"What's for supper?"

"Remember, dear, this is our hamburger night."

Edith was also elected president of our Saddle Creek Swim and Tennis board. This may mean that on Thursdays we have leftover hamburgers. Edie regularly visits my mother (who is back from the Health Center and doing well again in her own room at Wesley Woods). Edie is also Liz's tennis team mother, and she still plays a lot herself.

The result of all these efforts, both noble and entertaining, is that Edith has developed an advanced case of what she calls "Busy Brain." This is known as Information Overload in the computer industry and Gridlock in Manhattan. The most common and noticeable symptom is the loss of one's mind. It has caused Edith to do things like put Andy's sweater in the microwave instead of the drier. Really, she did. Luckily, Andy was already cooking a hamburger in it or we would have had V-Neck Flambé. Didn't this used to be called "senility?" Isn't this the earliest recorded case?

Trips in 1985: As part of her Bethel preparation, Edie spent a week this summer at a teacher training session in Madison, Wisconsin. Not only was it a terrific break for her just to get away, but the program was very inspirational and – she is sure – instrumental in her being chosen to teach this fall. Plus, she got to see the Blanchards while there – old Baldwinsville friends (well, not any older than we, I guess). Before that, in May, we all went again to Savannah for the Georgia All-State Chorus program. This year, both Andy and Liz made it – a double thrill for us. We had two wonderful weeks at Keuka Lake this summer at the Blocks', friends from church, and we got to visit with a number of upstate New York friends (we missed a few, but we'll be back). I don't think we've had as much fun or relaxation in a long time. Even Jen and Andy got off work for the second week, which we spent with the Matthaidesses.

Jennifer and Andy spent their 1985 spring break in Florida. Andy went to Daytona and Jennifer went to Ft. Lauderdale. When they first came up with the idea of "road-tripping," their plans were nice and simple: a few friends and a relaxing week on the beach. Well, as the time drew near, spring break segments were all over the news – the crowds, the traffic jams. I just knew the kids were going to have a terrible experience. To my surprise, they returned having loved "the crowds, the sun, the surf, and the parties." Ah, to be young again.

As for me, I just paid for all the stuff above. Oh, and I had my other toenail taken off so I wouldn't list to the right anymore. See last year's letter for more detail. While I was recuperating during Thanksgiving week, I laughed my way back to health with Lake Wobegon Days by Garrison Keillor. Funniest book I've ever read. You gotta get it! Andy, Edie, Liz, and I started a Folk Mass group at church this year which has been a lot of fun, a lot of work, but well received as our confidence grows. I trimmed the hedge by the mailbox and overseeded this fall. It doesn't take much to keep you happy as you enter your golden years.

I did take an interesting business trip to New York in the fall. On the way back, I was seated next to a real, authentic folk singer. My hero! I had taught myself to play the banjo in 1959 listening to Kingston Trio and Peter Paul and Mary records. (My sainted mother felt blessed that we had a huge house in which she and I could occupy opposite ends.) What a great opportunity to engage another professional musician in conversation. He was not interested in entertaining hero worshipers, however. Already on his second scotch and soda, he told me he was just waiting for the Percodan to kick in. Ah, fallen idols and broken dreams.

For the past few years, these letters have ended with Edie's little tip on child rearing or something, which I have always felt quite gratuitous, given the limited success we've had so far. Anyway, I have to admit that one of her tips has worked: Enforced Family

Outings. You may remember that these were designed by an adult (usually Edith) to make a person better or smarter or more cultured even if it was against his or her own will. Well, this fall, while at UGA for Parents' Weekend, Andy asked if we could all go to the Arts Center to hear the Atlanta Symphony Orchestra's Christmas program, as we had for the past several years. Edith slumped into a semi-coma, while I exclaimed, "You really want to go?" Edie ordered the tickets the next day. "See," she said, "EFO's really pay off!" Another major miracle in the Cobourn family.

We wish you miracles, too, and a joy-filled Christmas!

The Cobourns
110 Canter Court
Roswell, GA 30076
Christmas, 1986

Happy Holidays,

Merry Epiphany and Happy Groundhog Day! Yes, yes. We know. We're back to being late again this year. But we have an excellent excuse: we were sick. Knee-walkin', baggy-eyed sick. BIG TIME SICK! Strep, sinuses, separate bedrooms. Heavy illness. But we limped back to life just in time for another jam-packed Christmas.

Well, frankly, to get right to it, this year was not wall to wall fun: my mom on a waiting list for a less expensive nursing home; my sister Margaret's husband dying of cancer in February; unrest and anxiety at IBM as we struggle through business slumps and reorganizations; two in college; Edith going back to work to help pay for some of the above; and on and on. Not that the year had no lighter moments. Liz dropped Latin after a two-year struggle. "Gee, Dad, I just don't get it. Latin is like a foreign language to me."

And Edith, as you all know, is a lighter moment personified. She is working as an assistant teacher at our church's pre-school. She loves it! If for no other reason than it gives her good practice to be a grandmother (someday). Of course, she has had to revert to the mentality of the four-year olds she teaches. Now when I come home, I am greeted at the door with a song:

> *"Tony's coming in from work, in from work, in from work.*
> *Tony's coming in from work. Let's give him a hug!*

Look, Liz! Here's our DADDY! How was *our* day today, daddy?"

You probably get the idea.

Edie is still teaching her Bethel Bible Study. I think she's really hitting her stride, moving into her second year. She is now able to correct the sermons each Sunday. Last week, our minister was quoting Matthew's gospel, "This is my Son, with whom I am well pleased." Edith poked me and whispered, "that should be 'my beloved Son.'" Kinda makes you wonder how Moses and Peter and those other Bible guys got so far all by themselves.

But she's finally finished with her term as president of the Swim and Tennis Club. A private citizen again after two years – no more gala balls; no more secret service – and she got through it all without a maid. ("Beth Corey has a maid and she's only a committee chairman!") Anyway, thank God for Edie and her light moments. As the opening might indicate, without her I would be in the home myself by now.

The kids are all fine and all the same (the same as last year, and probably the same as yours) – going at top speed, pausing just long enough and just often enough to bring us just enough joy so we let them rev up to top speed again. When you're living in the fast lane, it sometimes takes you until 3am to slow down. They get mad at me for making so much noise (at 11:30am) that I wake them up. "One of the few times I get to sleep in, and Dad decides to clean out the fireplace with the ShopVac!" They are twenty-gasp-two, nineteen, and sixteen.

This year Jen and Andy rented a house with two other kids at Georgia. I resisted this idea for a long time as fundamentally un-American. They should live in a DORM like I did. That was not a particularly compelling line of reasoning for them. Oh, they were polite. After they cancelled their dorm contracts and signed the lease on the house, they forgave me and invited us up for dinner (bring your own steaks and salad fixings and sweet corn and beer and would you mind stopping on the way and picking up some charcoal and charcoal lighter oh and we don't have a spatula). Folks, the first time you are entertained by your children in their house is eerie! But it is certainly quieter than the dorm – and cleaner, too. Last year, Andy's roommate told us they let the rug go until it hurt to walk on it. THEN they vacuumed.

The highlight of Jen's year was her month in Colorado on the Young Life staff. She was a camper there as a high school sophomore and was selected to run the pool last summer. In no way could I describe this glorious experience of hers. Suffice to say, it was a sad and lonely flight back to Atlanta. The lowlight of her year was probably her Christmas break job at a funky clothing store at

Perimeter Mall. Hey! And how about those kids' fashions today? Those clothes are still B - A - G - G - Y........I have two daughters who look like Bedouin refugees. I made them stay in their rooms during the Libyan crisis so they wouldn't get stoned by the neighbors. BAGGY and B - I - G! If the shoulders don't go all the way to your elbows, it must've shrunk. Liz has one fetching army green "blouse" that is so big (how big is it, Johnny?) she could pitch it in the back yard and have a friend stay over. Haven't I been working 11 hours a day for 23 years so they could wear better clothes than that?

Speaking of Liz, she's also in overdrive – volunteering as a Candystriper; working as a cashier at a restaurant; and attending several sessions at Camp Mikell, our Episcopal Church camp in north Georgia. One of those sessions was something they call "Happening" – a youth renewal program (part of the Cursillo movement) that has made a profound impression on her. She will return this spring to work on the staff.

Liz is also trying out for the All-State Chorus again this year. All high school choristers in Georgia are eligible to apply. The kids must demonstrate voice and sight reading skills during regional tryouts, and only a couple of hundred are chosen from among the thousands who try out. Those selected are given the music to practice before the group rehearsal. The week before the scheduled program, they all gather in Savannah for practicing and partying (not necessarily in that order of importance). The concert is always spectacular, and we are amazed each year at the sound that talented high school kids can produce.

I've been trying desperately to think of some quirky things to tell you about Andy, and I'm having a real problem manufacturing something. Perhaps he's turning into a thoughtful, not-too-flashy, responsible guy like his Dad..............

Naaaaaaaaaaaaahhhhhhhhhhhh.

He does have a cute little girlfriend and he seems to pace himself better than Jen or Liz (or Edith, for that matter). He has developed into a superb musician. Andy and a friend made a demo tape this summer at a real recording studio. I love to play it for people and watch their reactions when they learn it's my beloved son, in whom I am well pleased.

And me? Heck. As Edie says, I'm gettin' to be just like a good Merlot: mellow and full-bodied. I was elected to the church vestry in November. I bet I'll have some fun stuff to tell you about *that* next year! I am becoming more domesticated now that Edith is working. I can put my own laundry away all by myself. She would tell you, however, that my training is a slow process. She sent me out last fall to buy $20 worth of goods for the Roswell food pantry for the poor. So I did. I got some regular stuff. Won ton soup. LeSeuer very young small early tender peas. Smuckers Rose Hip jelly. Grey Poupón mustard..... Well, you talk about critical! She was absolutely beside herself. How come I didn't get generic peanut butter and a 25 lb. bag of grits? I said what if there were some Yuppies in Roswell who had fallen on hard times? Do you expect them to have a tailgate party with peanut butter and no-name ginger ale? See, women just don't understand these things.

Mom fell and broke her hip in the spring. When she got out of the hospital and was ready to try to walk again, we discovered she was eligible for only four days of physical therapy from Medicare, even though she probably needed a month's worth at $400 a day. This is a bad time to have two kids in college. Since she'd had to exhaust her own funds before she was eligible for Medicaid, Mom had to begin using a wheelchair and could no longer be in a private room at Wesley Woods. The intermediate care unit there was $750 a month *more*, so we began to search for less expensive nursing homes. The most suitable one had a year's waiting list. What is wrong with this picture? We hope she'll be in the new place within a couple of months so we can go back to eating meals and using electricity.

Well, while the early part of '86 seemed to hold nothing but challenges, good news sneaked up on us toward year-end – the best of which came from IBM. Not onlt did I survive the latest reorganization, but I will stay in Atlanta, in a personnel function I love, working with people I respect and admire. Now that those prayers have been answered, we seek guidance for 1987 as to how Edie and I can lead the folk group together at church and still remain married. Stay tuned.

We send our love,

The Cobourns
110 Canter Court
Roswell, GA 30076
Christmas, 1987

Merry Christmas Y'all,

OK! 1988 New Year's Resolution number one: no more excuses about our late Christmas letter. I'm sick of screaming at Edith and making my own life miserable because she never gives me her input on time. My life is miserable enough these days and, as I approach my twilight years, I must concentrate on ways to "brighten the corner where I are"………so, whenever you get this, consider yourselves lucky and don't take us off your Christmas Card list.

It is December 22 as I begin this, and we were talking this evening, Edith and I, about Christmas presents – particularly those purchased by the younger family members, and more particularly about the cost distinctions they make between presents for boy(girl)friends and for family. We have a friend who one year noted the irony of her son's gift to a girlfriend of two weeks: a beautiful gold chain from Maier & Berkle Jewelers, while she herself got a lobster-claw potholder. This is the same kid who asked her, "Am I supposed to get Meemaw something, or what?"

Marginally more fortunate is our friend, Nora Butler, whose son bought her a neat bagel slicer for Christmas. Only when Nora got her VISA bill did it become clear that young Larry had only "picked out" her gift.

One would hope that our children's understanding of the TRUE meaning of the "Spirit of Giving" (i.e. the father is supposed to get the most stuff) would evolve as they mature. We shall see in a few days.

Well, let's catch up on the kids. Andy is a Junior at UGA this year, majoring in, like, English. He and Jen gave up last year's rented house and its associated roommate problems. Andy found an exquisite little basement apartment, so now only Jennifer has roommate problems. Andy's exquisite little basement apartment is about 9' X 12'. I told him Anne Boleyn had better living quarters.

We carefully planned his furniture arrangement on our 9' X 12' carpet and discovered that, in addition to the bed, he had the choice of a dresser, a chair, or a table. It turns out, though, that once you get a stereo, two guitars, and an amp in there, you have room for only the bed. So you see there is a fairly narrow range of activities available in Andy's room. The rest of his time is split between his girlfriend, Mary, studying, and his job. Guess which one takes priority.

His job, an immediate and welcome reaction to the October stock market plunge, is delivering pizzas in our 11-year old, 200,000+-mile wagon. So far, pizza delivery throughout greater metropolitan Athens has not caused the wagon to pass into that Big Junkyard In The Sky. Andy spent the last two weeks at work on crutches. He sprained his ankle when he fell out of a tree, while collecting mistletoe for a Christmas party Jen and her roommates were hosting. We wondered if Andy would make it to the party. Silly us! Crutches and all, he was there with Mary to assist when needed.

Liz is a high school Senior and is showing occasional signs of maturity and sensitivity. For example, we noticed earlier this year that her eyeballs were beginning to crust over. She was walking into walls and stuff. Seems she had failed to buy enzyme solution for her contacts. She said, "Well, I just hate to keep asking you guys for money." To which Andy replied, "Boy, if you're going to college, you gotta get over that!" Luckily, though, this aging process is evolutionary, and there are still flashes of the old Liz. She recently attended a U2 concert – with real good seats up front where the decibel level is well beyond the pain threshold.

"I was so close, Bono sweated on me!"

Since this letter is sent to very few teenagers, the less than fastidious Bono is apparently one of the U2 band members. Yuucchhhh!!!

She flew to Philly this spring to spend a long weekend with her buddy, Julie Prye. Just before boarding, Liz led us in prayer: "May I have a HUNK walk by, see the empty seat next to me and say, 'Hi. What's your name?' And I'll say, 'Well, sit down and let's talk about it.' Amen."

Liz's main school activity is still chorus, and she went to All-State again this year. This summer she spent lots of time at Camp Mikell in the North Georgia mountains as a church camp counselor. She's getting ready to apply to nursing schools now. Her mother thinks she'll be a good one because she's never had any trouble giving people the needle. Hmm, I wonder if I would have made a good nurse too.

Jennifer will soon complete her last quarter in college. HOORAY! She is more than ready to begin a new phase in her life, and we ask that you remember her in your prayers, so that that new phase will be: A JOB. Jen is also an English major, and the test case of my theory that businesses want to hire articulate and vivacious liberal arts graduates, not boring, one-dimensional specialists. Jen sure has had her fill of vacation jobs which are *not* what she wants to do for the rest of her life. This summer she was the supervisor of 15 pools with SwimAtlanta, a local pool maintenance company. She fixed pumps and fired lifeguards – then filled in for the guards she just fired because she couldn't find replacements. She learned all about the CURSE OF THE BEEPER this summer.

That job ranked right up there with root canal work. The pay was decent, though, and it enabled her to buy her first car: a '77 VW Rabbit (complete with bad brakes, bad shocks, and a brand new tape deck – a birthday present from her practical mother and father). She, too, took a trip to Philadelphia this year – that's still where her best friends are – and another to Austin for a party at UT with fellow counselors from her 1986 Colorado Young Life camp. Her most frequent activities now are: 1) being a bridesmaid in friends' weddings, and 2) doing leg lifts with Jane Fonda. In her transition to the "real" business world, she took a job this month with a temp agency. Her first assignment was helping an old lady get her house clean for Christmas. What's the starting salary range for Domestic Engineers?

And Edith? This was her Year Of Decision! First she decided to postpone her mastery of the computer and the "Managing Your Money" program until we find some actual money to manage. This will come no earlier than when the kids are out of college, and no later than when I die. Next, she decided to move up from assisting with the "older fours" to assisting the kindergarten teacher. This was a bold move – a decision made only after several agonizing family councils. She was to teach MATH! Edith would to have to learn addition and subtraction, but luckily only for numbers up to ten. So I supported her ambitious decision. She's doing great. What a gal! I guess she must be a born teacher. She graduated 14 from her Bethel Bible class this spring and began another class in the fall. She thinks she may begin to understand Genesis the third time through. She also started a new venture: Education for Ministry – a four-year course for lay people that covers the Bible, theological reflection, and church history. She loves it! I now make my own dinner Monday AND Wednesday AND Thursday night.

I'm searching the Bible for inspirational references on better hand/eye/mind coordination for Edith. Yes, she had another couple of "lapses" with the car again this year. We got a card last month from the Roswell Body Shop telling us that Edith is now eligible for their "preferred customer discount."

With no real family vacation this year (see "colleges" above), Edie went on every women's church retreat she heard about and called them mini-vacations. She also agreed to drive a friend's van as a "sag wagon" while the friend and her kids rode in the Bike Ride Across Georgia. This was billed as: "Serve a little Gatorade to the riders, see the Georgia countryside, catch a lot of sun, read a good book......." WRONGO, Adidas-breath! She fed Gatorade to 700 bikers in those funny tight suits, then ministered to the lame and the halt for the rest of each day – for seven days and 350 miles. No book, no sun, no leisurely countryside tour. This little escape, Edith says, was symptomatic of the "*worst* summer of my life" by which she means spending every day coordinating the use of the one remaining car (after mine and Jen's) among Andy, Liz, and herself. Three jobs, two summer school programs, one automobile. Edith swears she will NOT spend another summer standing at the back door waving good-bye to her car with someone else at the wheel.

Elsewhere in the family, my sister was here for a week at Labor Day. It was really great for Mom to be able to see her as Margaret cannot visit often. Her job with AT&T is going well; she has just gotten a promotion and has moved to a new office. We'll miss her this Christmas, but she'll be enjoying the holidays with her good friends in D.C.

Mom has settled in at A. G. Rhodes, the new nursing home she moved into in May. There are not as many "alert" companions as she had at Wesley Woods, but she likes the staff and we visit her frequently. She's still a big baseball fan (can you imagine a greater curse than being a baseball fan and living in *Atlanta*?) and she celebrated her 78th birthday in November.

My year was not nearly as humorous as that of the rest of the people who bunk here. There is still a lot of uncertainty about what my job with IBM is likely to be – a product of frenzied reorganizations caused by sagging revenues and intensified by my decision not to relocate to someplace where job choices might be more attractive. I promised some stories about my Vestry experience, but that's not a real yuk-it-up group. Actually, I resigned my post late in the year – a symbolic protest to the control-freak priest and his band of sycophants. If anyone believes the operation of a church is somehow more noble or democratic than, say, a SWAT team, come see me.

Let's see......my tennis team is funny to watch; and their wives come to cheer. We get all the winos and winettes out at the courts on Saturdays. We call ourselves a beer-drinking team with a tennis problem. One needs a thick skin to be on this team. If you happen to play well one match, you tend to make the other guys look bad. It's better when you stink; you're not as threatening to your teammates and they call out support from the sidelines:

"Don't worry, Dennis, you'll miss easier shots than
that!"
"Hey, Wob, it's time to wewease the secwet weapon,
but be vewy, vewy quiet."
"Yo, Frank, you guys look like Stevie Wonder and
Ronnie Milsap out there!"

And the ultimate shot at one of the guys who's a Delta pilot, and doesn't cover the court too well:

"Hey, Steve, the captain has turned off the seat belt
sign. You are free to move around now."

I guess the highlight of our year may have been our weekend at

Cursillo this fall. Although I was admittedly anxious about having somebody's idea of "spiritual renewal" thrust upon me for an entire weekend, those fears turned out to be unfounded. The whole program was wonderfully uplifting – a great comfort, it turns out, when life seems so demanding and expensive and unrewarding. So that experience has helped me to keep the faith. Hope you all have something like that to help you, too!

Have a wonderful Christmas and a blessed 1988,

The Cobourns
110 Canter Court
Roswell, GA 30076
Christmas, 1988

Merry Christmas,

This has been a year filled with celebrations, not the least of which is that this letter is being written (if not mailed) before Christmas.

In the spring, we celebrated my mother's participation in the annual A. G. Rhodes Nursing Home beauty contest. At first I was a little skeptical that this might be a farcical activity designed more for the amusement of the staff than for the enrichment of the residents. But mom and the other entrants were excited as they were elegantly coifed and dressed for the festivities. Andy and Liz and Edie were in the audience as I wheeled mom down the runway to face the questions from the cheesy-looking emcee, while an elderly pianist played music from the Forties. Mom was quick-witted and chipper as she told the audience she had won the prize for best legs in her last beauty contest – the 1930 Tri Delt house pageant at Syracuse University. We thought she was a shoo-in for Miss A. G. Rhodes, but she came in second. She was thrilled. Happy days are rare in nursing homes.

In June, we attended two graduations: Jen from college (she crammed four years into five – just like I did at Hamilton), and Liz from high school; both on the same day, 75 miles and one flat tire apart. Later that month we celebrated my 25th year with IBM, and, in September, Edie and I celebrated our silver anniversary – a period which we have described to many as 21 great years together! It was a memorable occasion, highlighted by a surprise party thrown by the kids. I remember when my sister and I did this for my parents' 25th and we forgot to invite several of their closest friends.......Bummer! No problem this time, though. Despite the absence of some far-away friends, it was a wonderful gathering. Thanks, kids!

Then Edie and I withdrew our last $50, took a trip to the Atlanta Zoo to see our favorite gorilla, Willie B., and had Chinese food on the way home. O.K., so it's not the trip to London we had originally planned, but the zoo does have a certain international aura. Besides, we had discussed a London vacation with the Matthaidesses. Although we both had enough frequent flyer points for the tickets, we had just enough cash to sit in Heathrow Airport for two weeks before returning home. Don't worry though. We'll get to London. When the Falcons win the Super Bowl. Well, OK, when the Braves win the World Series. Actually, Andy thought there was a special significance to celebrating 25 years of marriage at a zoo.

Speaking of Andy, he's a senior at Georgia – an English major. He thinks Emerson is a bore, but loves Poe (at least he did until he got his paper back!). Last year Andy had an "efficiency" apartment only slightly larger than our linen closet. He upgraded this year to a house, with some friends from freshman year. He traded his solitary lifestyle for three sloppy roommates. Poor Andy is the only one who cleans. Jen's reaction to this was, "There really is a God!" Jennifer, of course, has served as Andy's maid in various living arrangements here and at college. Anyway, Andy still consoles himself with his music, and he desperately needs a new amp and guitar so he can join a band at school. REM started this way – really – right there in Athens.

Liz is at Young Harris, a junior college in the North Georgia mountains. She loves it. She joined a sorority, the choir, the art league.........*and* almost joined the outing club, but I guess she decided to wait until winter quarter for that. We didn't see much of her this fall, even though she's only two hours away, so we anxiously awaited her arrival in November for Thanksgiving break. I asked her when she had to return to school. She said, "January 2nd!" Edie swooned.

All this time off allowed for her ambitious work plans – a banquet waitress at the Holiday Inn where "you can make $150 a night. Really, Dad." "Oh, good." Edie said. "Let's plan your Christmas earnings, Liz!" Edith LOVES to plan other people's money. Besides, Liz owed her $200. Needless to say (have you heard this before?), the Holiday Inn scheduled Liz for six nights out of the six-week period. And, by the way, the $150 a night is closer to $75. Anyway, Liz is still working toward a nursing career and her first year in college emptied our nest.

HA! Not so fast. Jen tricked us and moved back. Although I'm sure we were all a little anxious about that at first, we needn't have been. Edie and I really do love having her with us. Besides, it forced us to exterminate the cave crickets in her downstairs bedroom so the Fulton County Board of Health would lift its condemnation order.

Shortly after graduation, Jen heard about a group called English Language Institute/China (ELI/C), a Christian organization on the west coast which sponsors people to teach college English in China for a year. She applied and was accepted for the fall of 1989. To save for the trip, she is spending this year teaching 8th and 9th grade English at a private alternative school for kids with learning and behavior problems. She has had her hands full. Once, she was knocked unconscious by one of her more disruptive students. That is hardly unacceptable behavior today, though. Certainly the kid could not possibly be considered personally responsible – he must have been a victim of too little breast-feeding or too many M&M's or something. Why are all the great "learning experiences" painful? We keep telling her teaching in China will be HEAVEN compared to this.

This summer we headed north. Our first stop was Staunton, Va., one of Edie's childhood homesteads and birthplace of Woodrow Wilson. As we walked through town, she was overcome by the town's historical significance, and felt compelled to discuss other great events in history prior to her arrival there in 1952.

"Alright," she said, "in fourteen-hundred and ninety-two, Columbus sailed the ocean blue."

My eyes rolled back into my head. Edie was cracking up.

"Okay," she said, "then what happened?"

The trip ended with another wonderful family vacation at Keuka Lake – a week with the Matthaidesses and visits with many other upstate New York friends. Incredibly, all six kids from both families were there, although the young southern contingent arrived a little late. They started with a small detour to Norfolk, then broke a timing belt in Wilmington, then.......aw, never mind.

The trip also included my 30th high school reunion in Baldwinsville. The committee put on a program that was in much better taste than in previous years. They did NOT give their standard award for the oldest child to Nan Johnstone, the girl who couldn't say no. Nan, a grandmother now, was getting a little sick of this honor. Many of us have gotten really fat and slow. Memories of spearing frogs in the creek at One-Tree Hill with Jack Spring and Timmy Carter in the summer of '51 don't energize the conversation the way they used to.

Edith's medical bills will decrease in 1989 now that she has retired from teaching kindergarten. ("Now, wait a minute," I said. "I went to work first, and I should get to retire first.") Well, it was clear that this job was really beginning to disagree with her, so by the end of October she knew it was time to go. Anyway, her new freedom has made a remarkable difference in her outlook and has allowed her to concentrate on other areas of life – her Bethel Bible teaching, and her newest interest: GETTING ORGANIZED! Edith describes a lesson from her friend Laura Hayes as her "greatest Christmas gift." This lesson has yielded visible kitchen counters, a mail slot for each kid, and three new folders for Edith: Action, File, and Pending. The Pending file is 7 1/2 inches thick. I've always been secretly afraid of how dangerous Edith might be if she ever got organized. I think I may find out this coming year.

Her other greatest Christmas gift was a workshop at an Atlanta mental health hospital (No, wait. That's not the punch line. I'll let you know when it comes). The class was entitled "How to Like December." For years, her favorite week has been the week *after* Christmas and her favorite month, January. The message was to decide what's important at holiday time and throw the rest out. She had attempted this on her own a couple of years back by trying to eliminate stockings over the mantle, but Jen said, "NO!" So this year Edie's solution was to ask Jen to do the stockings. And Jen readily agreed. Wow! She wishes she'd taken this course long ago. (punch line)

Hope Santa fills your stockings with an extra measure of God's grace for the year ahead,

The Cobourns
110 Canter Court
Roswell, GA 30076
Christmas, 1989

Merry Christmas,

After last year's catalogue of anniversaries and graduations, we saved one celebration for 1989: my mother's 80th birthday. Although the setting wasn't as elegant as it might have been (the day room of the nursing home), the party itself was a great success and brought more smiles from mom than we'd seen in a long time. Andy and Liz were with us and Margaret came down from Manassas. She brought a huge album of letters she'd collected from mom's old college Fine Arts chums, Baldwinsville neighbors, and friends from all over. By the way, for those of you not yet in the "Sandwich Generation," here's how you do birthdays in a nursing home: CHEAP! Not because you don't love your mother, but because nice things tend to get "lost" somehow. K-Mart stretch pants are the answer.

As we mentioned last year, Jennifer was accepted into a program (English Language Institute/China) that provides English teachers for colleges in China. She spent the past year teaching and raising the required $10,000 for her trip. Although all the ELI/C teachers were sent home immediately after Tienanmen Square, the institute felt things were safe enough to return by fall. So, in early August, off she went to Zhengzhou University, about 400 miles southwest of Beijing. I'll let her tell you about her early adventures later.

With Jennifer gone, our nest is really empty. Luckily, though, it refills with Becky Drew, Jen's best friend from college, who drops in for dinner once a week. We love her company and that of our kids' other friends who come over to graze from time to time. A bunch visited before Andy returned to UGA. Three pans of lasagna – no leftovers. We ended the evening in the cul-de-sac, looking at the full moon, gaily trying to remember every "moon" song we ever knew. Remember, Edith and I are from an era when "moon" meant that big bright thing in the night sky and "gay" meant happy. Anyway, thank God for young adults! They keep us from atrophying.

Liz is a sophomore at Young Harris Junior College and is having a tough time because her roommate did not come back this year. She's still headed to nursing school next year, and she and Edie have been busy researching nursing programs. Liz barely survived her sorority's fall rush as one of the upperclassmen responsible for the pledges. Her suite houses the sorority president, social chairman, and pledge trainer, so the 30-plus pledges always seem to be lurking around her room. Sounds like she's taking after her older sister. Liz is delighted to have Jennifer's VW Rabbit while Jen is in China, but she'd rather have Jen back instead.

At the top of her Christmas list was "A visit to China to see Jennifer." We settled on a phone call – not an inconsequential expense, by the way. Communication with a third world country is both primitive and expensive. Mail to Jen takes forever and by the time it reaches her it has been opened and censored. Likewise, her mail to us is censored. She must be careful what she writes lest she come under the scrutiny of the university thought police. The apartment of one of the other teachers was bugged after her colleague was a little too open about her Christianity. Phone calls are also monitored, of course, but it's important to hear each other's voice from time to time. We have had some monthly phone bills reach $400. Here are some excerpts of Jen's letters from China:

8/3: (Diary) After arriving in California for training, I was told that if we knew all the struggles ahead, we probably wouldn't have come. (Oh, great; thanks a lot. Nice warning.)

9/2: (In China) Eleven-hour train ride from Beijing to Zhengzhou – had the wonderful opportunity to use a Chinese toilet – a hole in the ground (or in the train, I should say). Ros, a fellow teacher from Canada, and I share a two bedroom apartment with a small refrigerator (typical Chinese style) and no cooking facilities. Our "carpeting" is like the red carpet under the awning of a hotel. Upon arrival, we find a layer of silt on everything. It's loess – blown in from the desert. Reminds me of spring pollen season in Atlanta.

9/11: Everyone spells my name right here because they have no COBURN to confuse it with. (Dad, I think that's the only thing you would like here.) Sea slugs are a delicacy in China. I haven't had the pleasure. And, Dad, dog is only eaten in south China.

9/21: (Christmas list) Refrig. magnets, sachets (anything that smells good), duct tape, glue sticks, a tape from the family (talk to me, please!), anything American!!

9/26: I'm going to be on Chinese TV! A 15-minute film which explains foreign experts (that's us) in Henan province. Most families here have TV. They don't have sponges, but they have TV. You figure it out. Mr. Peng, our Waiban (in charge of us), is who asked me to do the film. Mr. Peng is a geek/spaz personified. He spits when he talks. For some reason, he likes me. I am getting used to him.

10/1: I got your package with FOOD in it. I am cherishing every Pepperidge Farm pretzel. (Little things float my boat lately.) Thank you. Thank you. Thank you. (Chinese fashion: say everything three times.)

10/9: Everything here takes so much time. To do a load of laundry takes 45 to 60 minutes, not counting hanging to dry.

10/14: As I'm writing to you, Spot, my lizard, is crawling above my bed. I'm thinking about putting him/her down in the kitchen for a while now that I have his/her babies to keep me company. The excitement never ends around here!

11/15: I just got the news that John Block died in a car wreck right after his graduation from Ga. Tech. I just sat and cried. I can't believe it! My heart just hurts for his family. Within a week one friend gets engaged and another dies, and I'm in China not able to celebrate or mourn with anyone. These are times I feel most alone. But when I put it in perspective, living here is easy as I think of what the Blocks have suffered this year.

11/20: I'm sick again! Ros has it too. Don't worry, though. By the time you get this, we'll both be healthy again.

11/27: Sara and I just saw a guy with a real (non-polyester) sweatshirt! It was too cool and now we both want one. So now I have to use my guanxi (connections) and see if the unit will sell us one. Dad, I want to hear some new jokes. Tell Mr. Bell I'll get him some cute little Chinese gift if he comes up with a joke that makes me laugh hard over here.

Wo ai ni (I love you)
Jennifer

Edith is not working and not teaching Bethel. She's had an interesting year trying to determine what direction her life will take now that her career as a mother is winding down. After a year in the slow lane, she thinks this may be her speed. "Be still and know that I am God" is her motto. I'm not sure she could get any stiller. I came home the other night and put a mirror to her lips to see if there was breath.

On a sad note, Edie has still not heard from her sister, Martha, in several years. She had contact for a little while after Martha moved out in 1983, but has lost touch since then. Martha was in the Ansley Park area of Atlanta for some time, but she has apparently moved. I hope they're able to get together again, as Edie has no other immediate family remaining and is feeling rootless. Edie thinks about her often, and is poignantly reminded of this loss every Christmas when Diana Wolff, the third member of their European jaunt in 1960, writes to ask, "How's Martha?"

Edie has used some of her spare time taking a few college courses, the first being World History – early Civilizations. She'd been dying to know whether there was anyone in China when the Apostles were hanging around Jerusalem.

We send you our love and prayers,

The Cobourns
110 Canter Court
Roswell, GA 30076
Christmas, 1990

Merry Christmas,

Jennifer is back in China. Her original arrangement with ELI/C was to teach for one year in Zhengzhou. But, like many of her fellow teachers, she was fascinated enough by this adventure that she re-upped. The decision forced her to come home for the summer and raise more money for the upcoming year. Jen spent her time giving slide shows and cooking Chinese food for small groups of prospective donors. We soon learned to disable the smoke alarm *before* she started cooking. Chinese use very hot wok!

After a successful money-grubbing campaign, she took off again at the end of the summer for Asia. Several of her co-workers and pals are going back too, and Jen is looking forward to a year in which adjustments to the third world lifestyle are not quite as startling as they were the first time around.

The good news about this extension is that Edie and I will visit her in February! We saved the frequent flyer points from the anniversary trip to London we couldn't afford in 1988 and are using them now to fly to China. Chinese New Year is a multi-week celebration, so ELI/C has an annual teachers' conference in Hong Kong. We will spend a few days with Jen there, then venture onto the mainland. We'll probably visit Shanghai and Beijing, then return with her to school in Zhengzhou. This should be especially exciting for me as the only foreign country I've ever visited is Canada. (Well, I did travel to Vassar and Skidmore a couple of times when I was in college.) I wonder if you can get Molsons and Labatts in China.

In June, Andy left Athens and his band, The Smash Fantastic, to return to the real world. I had threatened to buy him a sweatshirt that proclaimed: "The University of Georgia: The Best Five or Six Years of Your Life." Within a matter of weeks, he had been transformed from long-haired rock star to Princeton cut, tie-and-shirt-clad employee of Arthur Andersen. He's finishing up his last course at Georgia State and will get his degree from UGA next spring.

Andy's living with his friend, Brian Ivey, in Brian's Roswell cottage and commuting daily to downtown Atlanta. I have the pleasure of meeting him for lunch from time to time. Both Andy and Brian play guitar, so Andy has not strayed far from the music scene. He presented us with a tape of his compositions this Christmas – *Homemade*.

Liz returned from Young Harris in March, feeling she'd spent enough time there. She was having difficulty with her studies and has been diagnosed with a learning disability, so she'd had about as much academic fun as she could stand. For the next five months, she waitressed in a Mexican restaurant – earning mucho dinero – and is now enrolled at Brenau College in Gainesville, GA. Brenau has a learning center designed to help with Liz's auditory processing deficit. Finally, at 20, Liz is learning how to learn! Guess what? It works. Liz had a 3.6 GPA the first quarter.

Liz is a Phi Mu pledge, so everything she wears now is pink with Greek letters. She told Edith she needed some new sweatshirts. Edie suggested one Phi Mu sweatshirt and one Brenau. "Two sweatshirts for three more years of college? Gah, mom, get a life!" Edith still has the one Syracuse U. sweatshirt she wore throughout her four years. She agrees that she needs a life, though, and she hopes our newly emptied nest will provide a suitable one.

Edie felt the need to move out of the slow lane she was in last year and went to work for Currey and Co., a funky little home furnishings store in town which sells everything from garden benches to southern folk art. Customers feel free to bargain ruthlessly in stores like this and the sales tactics Edie honed there paid off handsomely at Christmas when she bought a $40 tree for $25.

We had a couple of spiritual renewals this year. After eight years at our local church, and our priest's pig-headed refusal to support Jennifer's mission, we found a new parish 22 miles north, near Lake Lanier. We know, we know. You're not supposed to shop for priests. But you're not supposed to groan through the sermons every week either. Sam Candler, the rector at Holy Spirit in Cumming, is young and thoughtful and kind and inspiring. He was a music major in college and the liturgy is wonderful. We needed feeding. It's worth the drive.

Not content with simply improving our church experience, Edie signed us up for a marriage retreat in August at a center on Lake Martin in Alabama. Oh, great. More sensitive relationships. More sharing. More honest communication. I thought the sharing we did between innings of the Braves games was sufficient, but Edie was apparently looking for something more.

She persevered with this plan even though she had heard about one couple who split up after such intense self-examination. Cynical old me! It turned out to be a wonderful week: great fellowship, great food, and really great insights for better marriages. Guys can't win at these things, though. It seems you're supposed to practice the new relationship techniques *afterwards* too – not just during the retreat. Oh, well.

In addition to my spiritual reawakening, I plowed new intellectual ground. I had adapted a module on business ethics based on IBM's management training practices and presented it to a group of MBA candidates at Emory University. Emory's students are a mix of recent undergraduates and experienced business people. Ethics is an art, not a science, and the discussions we had on this topic were fascinating. Think about the moral dilemma in the mind of a cigarette manufacturer who tries to maintain his employees' job security and his shareholders' investment by increasing his exports to unsuspecting customers in Asia and Africa. Or a manager's anguish when he finds his most productive and essential employee has submitted fraudulent expense accounts to pay for experimental surgery that restored his daughter's vision.

That gig led to similar guest appearances at Georgia State and Brenau College, where I was introduced as an Adjunct Professor! I'm sure my kids will soon begin to treat me with more respect. They should. They already know how good I am at lectures.

Here's a trivia question: How many car wrecks/citations/ oopsies has Edie had since we began these Christmas letters in 1973? Not so fast. She totaled the Toyota this year. The good news is that it was NOT HER FAULT! In fact, the other driver, having broadsided her into a median, was unnerved when she emerged with a huge grin on her face. She couldn't wait to get home to tell me she had *finally* had an accident for which she was not responsible. The Toyota wasn't so happy. It looks as if Edith will be using her newly acquired negotiating skills at the car dealer.

Please keep us in your prayers from February 7 through March 5. We hear that traveling independently in China is very difficult, but Jennifer says it's the only way to see the real country. By the way, mail from the U.S. is <u>priceless</u> to Jennifer, even though it's heavily censored. If you'd like to send her something that will *not* be censored, we'll be glad to act as couriers. Get it here by February 6.

Have a wonderful holiday,

The Cobourns
110 Canter Court
Roswell, GA 30076
Christmas, 1991

Merry Christmas,

I can't believe that at this time last year I was buying a money belt and a bra stash in preparation for our February trip to China. (The bra stash was for Edie. I am no longer into that sort of thing.) What an incredible journey! When Jennifer came home after her first year, she told people China could not be described; it had to be experienced. She was right. We saw it, felt it, tasted it, and smelled it. Whew! We thank God for having been able to share that with her.

I *tried* to describe it in my journal, though. If I missed you in the distribution, let me know. Edie kept a journal, too, but she declined to submit hers for publication. Too many relational experiences: who is not speaking to whom, why, and for how long. Twenty-four hour togetherness is a true test. We missed Liz reminding us "not to get our panties in a wad!" Well, the spats weren't *my* fault. If only **once**, Edith or Jennifer had worried about being on time for the next plane/train/whatever…. But Edie said, "One whiny, uptight, anxiety-ridden member of the group is enough."

Ah, testy memories dim, however. We'll probably do something like this again sometime. Edie yearns to see the Holy Land, India, Tibet, etc. I just want to go somewhere with flush toilets and ice cubes. We'll see.

The week of our departure began badly. We were scheduled to leave on Thursday. Monday morning I got a call at work that my mother had died unexpectedly at the nursing home. She'd had a stroke. We knew she had been upset about the prospect of our being away for a whole month, but we had arranged for her to be supplied with cigarettes and visitors. Nevertheless, as the nursing home aides suggested, she "picked her time."

Our mourning period was brief – both because our trip could not be rearranged and because, frankly, her life had lost most of its luster at the nursing home. We were sad to lose her, but not sad that she would no longer be in that dreary place with its confused residents and harried staff. It must be terrible, as your once-vibrant life winds down, to be alert yet discouraged by your physical limitations; lots of memories and no one to share them with except family a couple of times a week.

The end of the China trip demonstrated that Edith can sleep anywhere, anytime. After our 15-hour return flight from Hong Kong, Edie was sick and tired. With a 4-hour layover in San Francisco, she checked out the floor of the crowded Delta terminal. It was carpeted and (relatively) clean – something we had not seen in a month. With her backpack as a pillow and a coat over her head, Edie plopped down on the floor for a snooze. I was, of course, mortified, poking her frequently, whispering that she looked like a bag lady, threatening to move her over a vent and put her luggage next to her in a shopping cart.

Then it was back to IBM for me and back to selling patio furniture for Edith – right at the peak of the season: March through May. (On March 17, in honor of St. Patrick, the store renames its product "Paddy O'Furniture." Ha ha. Get it?) In April, just as Edie was learning to distinguish all-weather wicker from garden teak, the owner announced the store was closing. The sales staff's incentive to stay to the bitter end was increased commissions that would make them rich.

The going-out-of-business period was the WORST experience of Edie's many careers. She became a common laborer – hauling tables and unloading trucks. She pacified obstreperous customers who threw themselves onto the merchandise they wanted, then *screamed* for sales assistance. Her sweet "Christian" co-workers turned avaricious as they elbowed her aside to get to the customers first. Edie pouted as she hid in the bathroom, then complained at night about her paltry commissions.

Edie's unemployment would be a blessing in disguise, however, as Jennifer finished her second year in China, and came home in July. We were delighted to have her back and were looking forward to a more normal relationship as she readjusted to the U.S. culture and started looking for a job or a date or whatever. Boy, did she fool us!

Just before our February landing in Asia, Jennifer had met a young man through a fellow ELI/C teacher. His name is Ray Tse, a Hong Kong native who had gone to college in Seattle. Ray and Jen met us at the airport and Ray was our tour guide while we were in Hong Kong. A romance blossomed that spring and, within six weeks of Jen's arrival home, she missed Ray so much she decided she had to return to China to find out if she was really in love. She needed only two things: the money to fly back and a job so she could stay there.

"Dad, could you *please* lend me the money for the ticket? I *know* I'll get a job right away and I'll pay you back." I did and she did and she did. She has a P.R. job with a German clothing company that makes linings, interlinings and waddings for American accounts like Liz Claiborne and The Gap.

Edith decided that our foray into China was not enough adventure for one year, so she planned a July raft trip down the Ocoee River with our friends, the Fords. Having closed my eyes during several scenes in "Deliverance," I offered to meet the three of them at the end of the run with sandwiches and cold beer, but they insisted they needed my company.

White water rafting is a full contact sport. The guides prepare you carefully with helmets, life jackets and instructions:

"If you fall out, don't panic; chances are, we'll pick you up right away. Right, Eric?"

"Yep, heh, heh; haven't lost anyone yet, have we Mark?"

"What about those two guys who had heart attacks in 1988?"

"No, no, I mean people who drowned and we couldn't find 'em; anyway, if we don't get you right away, ride on your back with your feet pointed down river and your knees tucked under your chin. DO NOT try to stand up! Your foot may get caught between the rocks and the current will suck you under and you will die a horrible and agonizing death!"

Now, like Winnie-the-Pooh, I am a "bear of very little brain," but this was beginning to sound riskier than brain surgery. We donned our gear and tumbled into the raft. Luckily, they had opened a dam upstream, so we were to be blessed with some serious rapids. Within three minutes, both Edith and I were tossed out when another raft bumped us in some class 4 rapids. The guide chose to save Edith, but called out to remind me not to try to stand. I tucked up and floated downstream, scraping bottom, trying to breathe. It seemed like forever and I knew I would die. Edith had recovered enough by now to begin screaming. People in another raft grabbed for me. And missed. I took in a breath and sucked water.

My life didn't really pass before my eyes; and I didn't see people in white robes, backlit by heaven's aurora, but I did wonder about what I had last said to Edith. I knew it wasn't "I love you." But was it kind? And what about the kids? When did I last talk to the kids? God, I can't **breathe!!!!!**

Finally, the guide in a third raft threw a rope over my shoulder. I grabbed it with the last of my strength and held on as they pulled me in. I lay in the bottom of that raft for ten minutes, inhaling life and thanking God for another chance. Our raft pulled up alongside and I glimpsed the terror in Edie's eyes. Neither of us was having a really good time. She and the Fords helped me transfer back and I tried to look chipper as we began the rest of the trip.

Within fifteen minutes Edith was out again. We got her quickly, though, and she and I sat in the raft bottom for the rest of the ride, figuring out how much money we had blown to have this much fun. We decided we hadn't spent enough so we bought a couple of t-shirts to commemorate our adventure. My t-shirt shows off the scars on my arms.

Andy will be an official college graduate at the end of this quarter and is trying to decide on his life's calling. The corporate world is not for him. He thinks he may get a teaching certificate and he's working at a new restaurant in town so his days are free for classes. Life's calling may still be the arts. He's continues to write songs and play guitar, but he has also been working with friends recently, writing a TV parody they're trying to sell to the Fox network. It's a game show they've entitled, "Whose Fart is This, Anyway." Zany stuff. Watch for it soon and play along with your friends. (Whose fart was that? Roseanne Barr's or Jimmy Carter's?) Hey, it's a living.

Liz is home for the year, working at the same new restaurant as Andy and saving money for nursing school. She was not too thrilled at Brenau last year. No guys. Hey, if you're not thrilled at an expensive private college, you're outta there! Her decision came too late to transfer, so she's moved into the Jennifer Cobourn memorial suite downstairs. Liz is saving for a new car, too, and she and her mother shopped for one till they dropped this fall. Edie had honed her purchasing skills earlier on her own car, and she was razor-sharp by the time she and Liz went looking. The first one they found blew an engine during their test drive and they took it back to the dealer on a tow truck. They finally bought a sporty little Toyota SR-5 – just right for Liz's budget and lead foot.

Edith moved deftly from employment to unemployment to employment again – now as a real estate appraiser working for a church friend in north Georgia. On weekdays, she tramps around in duck boots and jeans evaluating everything from $650,000 starter mansions to ramshackle chicken houses (never say "coops" to chicken farmers). On Sundays, she's in church, teaching adult bible classes and has coerced me into attending this year's program: Kerygma.

I have successfully avoided bible studies for fifteen years, but Edie promised I could be poet laureate of this class. One Old Testament lesson required us to create a psalm proclaiming the virtues of Samuel. Here's my psalm which will probably be in the next revision to the Book of Judges:

> Samuel, oh Samuel, you Israelite animuel,
> Your mama was faithful old Hannah.
> You all lived in Canaan, where it's always rainin'
> On crops, so you never need manna.
> Your mama gave you to the Lord, it is true,
> To take over the land that you trod.
> So listen to Eli; on him you can rely.
> Go out and kick butt for God.

Bible study is a great respite from tense days at IBM. With projected cuts of another 20,000 next year, our managers are having a tougher time persuading the less productive people to take voluntary incentives to resign or retire. It's a good thing President Bush has certified there's no recession or things might *really* be bad around here!

Lately, a lot of my time is spent training managers how to fire people. This is not a spiritually fulfilling way to make a living. Anyway, it's hard to be clinical about your job when close friends are beginning to be affected by economic reality.

We are anxiously awaiting the arrival of Jen and Ray for Christmas. After two years in China, Jen is PSYCHED about a Christmas at home. Hope you are psyched about the holidays, too.

We send you our love and prayers,

The Cobourns
110 Canter Court
Roswell, GA 30076-1013
Christmas, 1992

Merry Christmas,

Tsk. Tsk. Late again. At least I *started* this before Christmas with the following line: "We're approaching Christmas in Atlanta and, as I begin this year's letter, it is 77°. Of course, with the wind chill factor, it feels like 72°."

Anyone who has looked at the enclosed Christmas Card has already guessed our biggest news for 1992: Jennifer's marriage on June 6 to Ray Tse! Since they live in Hong Kong and the wedding was in Roswell, all the planning was long distance. Jennifer and Edith reached out and touched each other at least once a week (at about $50 a touch). Most of the plans were executed by Edith. So much for that special mother-daughter bonding during wedding preparations. Nevertheless, it was a glorious occasion. Aren't they all?

Liz lost beaucoup pounds in order to rival her sister for most beautiful participant. Jen arrived home two weeks prior to the wedding – plenty of time to take part in the inevitable last minute crises, the largest of which was the *final* wedding dress crisis. The first wedding dress crisis occurred when Jennifer decided to wear her mother's dress. Edith was not sure that was a good idea and tried to talk her out of it. I jumped for joy over the extra money that could now be invested in extra bourbon at the reception. **NOT!** After the restoring, altering, beading, and preserving *of a dress we already* **owned,** *for crying out loud,* it was back to a BYOB reception plan. The final dress crisis came after the last fitting. The sleeves *still* weren't right. Corrections were hastily made and the dress was delivered at 11:30 on the morning of the ceremony.

For you fathers who have yet to experience the planning of a wedding, I have begun a support group especially for you. Call 404-962-5919 now. If you are already in the middle of wedding plans, you may have a loved one call for you. That's 404-962-5919. Operators are standing by.

The whole thing turned out fine. We had bourbon at the reception after all. Anyone who had not exhausted his or her tears at the wedding had another chance at the reception when we gave Jen and Ray a musical sendoff. When Jennifer decided she needed to go back to Hong Kong last year, I wrote a song about how little time we would have together and titled it, "Before You Go Away." Andy, Liz, and I sang it at the reception, backed up by Andy's guitar, my banjo, and the dance band. It had the desired effect.

One week after the wedding, we joined Jen and Ray back in Hong Kong for the <u>Chinese</u> celebration. In the Chinese tradition, both families must be represented at a wedding, and it was a lot easier (and cheaper) for us to travel there than for Ray's large family to come to the U.S.

The trans-Pacific plane ride was long, as usual, and Edie started in early with her GREAT IMPONDERABLE QUESTIONS:

Nudge. "Oh, look, Tony. What river is that?"
"Where are we?"
"I don't know."
"Then it's either the Chattahoochee or the Platte or
the Colorado. It's too early for the Yalu."

I have finally learned how to deal with Edith's GREAT IMPON-DERABLES. When she says, "I wonder how many homes were in that subdivision back there," I simply respond, "I wonder."

Hong Kong was crowded, as usual, but Jen and Ray's apartment in Quarry Bay was an unexpected oasis in that teeming city. It's quite spacious, especially for two, and has a spectacular mountain view. How teeming is the rest of the city? Let's say there's an average of five people to an apartment – 1,000 sq. ft. or less – four apartments to a pod, five pods to a floor, 30 floors to a building, 10 buildings to a complex, four complexes in the Quarry Bay area, and who knows how many such areas in the entire city. It's back to back and belly to belly!

We are awed by the difference in background between our daughter and son-in-law, and how they found so much in common that they fell in love. True, Ray attended college in the U.S. and has had many years to adjust to western society, but his roots will always be in the East. Jennifer's three years in China and Hong Kong have helped her appreciate those roots. Jennifer has always had her own room in our four-bedroom, 2 1/2-bath houses. Ray never had more than 54.5 sq. ft. to call his own. They catch each other by surprise sometimes.

While in the Far East, we had a wonderful vacation on Koh Samui, a primitive little island off the east coast of Thailand. As you would guess, our trip there was eventful. I should have been prepared for trouble when I saw our flight was booked through Shoestring Travel, Ltd. Once there, we had a very relaxing four days. Despite the herd of water buffalo on our "beach," we found places for snorkeling, swimming, and hiking, and had lots of Thai noodles, tom yum soup, and Singh Ha beer. The topless beach where all the German girls go wasn't a bad diversion either. If your support group helps you survive the wedding, this is a great place to wind down.

Well, there's still a lot of turmoil at IBM. The purges are becoming more frequent and I'm spending an increasing amount of time helping managers develop selection criteria for layoffs. We're cutting deeper and deeper, and the incentives to leave are not nearly as generous as they once were.

Our first program, in 1986, was strictly voluntary. If you agreed to resign or retire, you got two years pay spread over the next four years. And if you worked at one of three specific plants, you also got a $25,000 bonus to leave! If your job went away at the plant and you didn't want to leave, we'd try to find you a comparable position in another department. If we had to move you into a lower level job, we did not reduce your salary. In fact, the next raise you got was at your former level's range. If we could not find a suitable position in the plant, you'd have priority selection of the jobs for which you were qualified throughout the U.S. If you weren't qualified for jobs for which there were openings, we'd pay to retrain you, then pay to move you there, again at the same salary as your old job. This process applied to secretaries and clerical workers as well as to senior staff and management.

We had one interesting case of a college recruit from Duke. He was hired on a Friday to be an engineer at our Boca Raton plant.

The following Monday, we announced drastic cuts at Boca. We gave our Duke recruit two choices: a similar job at our Raleigh plant or the same deal we were offering our Boca employees: two years pay plus $25,000. Guess which one he took? When I think of friends who've been laid off from GE and other places, at least IBM is doing this with as much style and grace as possible.

Andy and Liz are now living and working in downtown Atlanta. They rented a house in the Georgia Tech area and are grateful for both the independence and the ten-minute drive to work. Andy is still pursuing his musical career, sustaining himself temporarily as a cook and bartender at The Point, an Atlanta café which features live bands. The job is lucrative but the clientele tends toward white clown-face makeup and all-black clothing of an unknown genre. "Bohemian?" asks Edie. "Gothic," says Andy.

Liz is waitressing at the Stein Club, a natural step in her quest to be a nurse. She will take a certified nursing assistant course in January, hoping for a hospital job which will allow her to study for her R.N. Her new post-wedding body now craves the very vegetables which it formerly considered yucky and she righteously disdains the slabs of red meat I am known to consume.

Liz and Andy visited Jennifer and Ray in Hong Kong this fall and journeyed into China, getting to see Beijing and Zhengzhou. They viewed many of the same spectacular sights we had seen, and discovered, as we had, that a trip to a third world country isn't exactly a "vacation." Their return to Hong Kong began with a 29-hour train ride from Zhengzhou to Guangzhou (Canton). Despite the cramped quarters, this environmentally conscious duo had been careful to save their trash for proper disposal at the end of the grueling trip. As they pulled into the station, the attendant came around to pick up the trash. Andy and Liz looked on, horrified, as he opened their compartment window and threw the trash onto the platform! Oooohh, we can't wait to see what China does to Hong Kong after 1997.

Edith achieved a grade of 88 in her Real Estate Appraiser course this fall – the course from hell: economics, banking, and real estate. Six weeks later she "retired" (again!), convinced that this is not her field. By the time she had earned her license, she thought, I would be retired myself, ogling young buns in Florida, while she and her tape measure tromped through north Georgia measuring chicken houses (never say coops) and lake homes.

Actually, Edith never really retires. She just retires from getting *paid*. She immediately stepped up her volunteer activities: adult Bible study teacher, Christian Education coordinator, church Vestry member, Swim & Tennis club board, etc. to go along with planning the wedding and planning Enforced Family Outings during homecomings at Thanksgiving and Christmas. God forbid that a moment should pass without an activity or three in Edith's life. Just recording it all gives me the vapors. Better quit.

We hope you had a blessed holiday season and wish you a happy, prosperous New Year,

The Cobourns
110 Canter Court
Roswell, GA 30076-1013
Christmas, 1993

Merry Christmas,

It's Christmas again! It must be. The salad shooter ads have begun. Actually, this year Sam's Club displayed its singing Christmas tree lights just before Labor Day, I think, which means I was sick of "Jingle Bell Rock" by Halloween instead of by Thanksgiving when I'm usually sick of it.

This will be a very different Christmas for us since we will spend it in Seattle with Jen and Ray. But then, it's been a very different year. First of all, I retired from IBM in August. Thirty years and a generous "golden handshake" and I'm OUTTA HERE! Retirement means plenty of free time. You can stand at the cash register in the grocery store, arranging all your currency to face the same way in descending sequence, while holding up the folks behind you who are late getting back to work.

Your wife thinks you now have time to "share" the responsibilities that have been rightfully hers since the Kennedy administration. For example, you get to make all your own appointments. ("This is Dr. Cohen's office manager, Angie O'Plasty, and you have been answered by our obnoxious message routing system. If you would like to make or change an appointment, press 1 now. If you are having a heart attack or stroke, press 2 now. If you are flatulent or hyperacidic, press 3 now ... ")

You have time to watch ALL the ads on TV – ads which give detailed attention to things like perspiration, incontinence, and baldness, then solve your problems in fifteen seconds with Speed Stick, Depends, or spray-on black hair). Or, you can avoid the ads by watching nature shows on PBS. A retired friend of mine has, since 1987, watched animals of every known species copulate on educational TV. I am not making this up!

Actually, I'll be only semi-retired. I have started my own business: Anthony's Premium Fudge; cream and butter fudge poured into packages that are then shrink-wrapped for freshness. I hope to sell the fudge next year through local retailers. I now have my own UPC bar code, 30,000 elegant labels, some terrific packaging, a new PC, 367 pages of government regulations, and a unique marketing idea. I expect to incorporate soon. All I need now is customers. Naaaaahhh, I'll get them after New Year's. Getting this all started is too much fun to worry about silly old customers. I will probably become a thousandaire very soon. That will be a good thing; otherwise, we will remain independently poor, thus eliciting a visit from Hillary Rodham Clinton or Janet Rodham Reno.

We think we are empty nesters for good now. That is to say, Edith has turned the Maytag down to "small load." You never know, though. Kids are sneaky. And the nest, of course, is in various stages of disrepair. I'll probably fix it up after my nap.

The last to leave the nest was Liz. Here are excerpts from her 1993 contribution:

"I've realized that I have no idea what the future holds for me. That's a scary thought for a 23 year-old who has just moved to Seattle thinking she had her life in order. At the beginning of this year, I couldn't shake the itch to travel. So … I quit my job, sold my car, gave my puppy away, packed up all my belongings, and headed west with several friends and 30 lb. backpacks.

"Telluride, CO, and the bluegrass festival was a blast! Then on to Utah, ending up in Bozeman, Montana. I did this trip with guys because of the strenuous backpacking and mountain biking. Basically, I became one of the guys – hairy legs and all! But three weeks in Bozeman was all I could stand before I had to head further west alone to my 'new family' in Seattle: Jen and Ray! Being closer to Jen and getting to know Ray better was my first reason for moving here. My second was to finish school and third was to find the Christian community I've been looking for in my age group. The Lord has blessed me with all three – and a good job! I am at Seattle Pacific University and have abandoned my quest for nursing. I may write my own major – to include Psych, Social Services, and Theater. Hmmm. I wonder where that will put me in the workplace. Musical comedy for the homeless? Anyway, I miss living with my great brother and singing with him in Atlanta, but I know God has led me here for a reason. (A man, maybe?)

Love, Elizabeth"

Liz's departure left Andy alone in a downtown Atlanta house that was now twice as expensive as he'd bargained for, so he quickly found two new roommates (Meg Ryan's brother and sister) and a house much closer to work. Andy's VW bug, which has black lung disease in addition to its several melanomas, was very appreciative. Andy's world is still the Atlanta music scene. For those of you whose last music scene was Perry Como and Theresa Brewer, it is different now. You need an update. Recently, the Cotton Club featured Hillbilly Frankenstein, whose music is described by the Atlanta Journal/Constitution as "cramps-like psychobilly."

At the Wreck Room you can see Snake Nation, Vinyl Banana, Vagrant Justice, Spot, Psycho Betty, and Standard Fruit. (I wonder if Psycho Betty is Spot's owner..... or mother.) PJ's Nest showcases Horse Hockey and Gunther's Growth. And at Andy's place, The Point, the featured act is Morphine. The paper describes this group as a hypnotic rock trio. I suspect so. The paper describes The Point as a "human zoo." I suspect so, too. Andy is still keeping several options open: working on a CD, thinking about forming a band, considering going on the road with another group – all while continuing to write inspired music, including a new song about his sister Elizabeth.

In June, as Liz already indicated, Jen and Ray moved to Seattle from Hong Kong (25 hours closer to Atlanta, for those of you who think of Seattle as far away). Edie went house hunting with Jen in April and both got to explore that unique city. They said the views of water and mountains are incredible, if you are patient enough for the weather to clear. While they were graciously hosted by the Burrs, Ray's Seattle family, I got to stay home and read Edie's "don't-forget-to-eat-your-vegetables" notes. Bachelorhood is quiet,

101

the answering machine being the only other conversationalist in the house. Cashews are vegetables and there's a lot of fiber in beer. You don't need the dishwasher anymore and you eventually just ignore the unmade bed. I managed.

Jen and Ray bought a new house on Queen Anne Hill, just a few minutes from downtown and in the neighborhood of Seattle Pacific University, where Ray went to college and where Jen is now taking courses toward a teaching certificate. Ray is busy establishing contacts to transfer his small electronics importing business to the States. It's slow going, but he's optimistic and ambitious. Jen came to Atlanta in July to sort through several decades of her "stuff," loading much of it – plus several boxes of Elizabeth's memorabilia – onto a rental truck in which she and Andy headed west. They got across the swollen Mississippi just in time to miss the terrible floods and saw a lot of this country's beauty along the way. Andy did most of the driving. Jen shut her eyes going up and down the mountains.

The Tse's big news is that we will become GRANDPARENTS next May. Yikes! (Remember the old Malvina Reynolds folk song? "Where are you goin' my little one, little one?.....Turn around and you're a young wife with babes of your own.") Well, we're ready. Jen has had a rather sickly three months so far and her condition, we hope, will improve soon. But while this may not be easy for her, we think it will be easy for us. You just put the money you used to spend on college into the "baby gift" budget category and.......... Despite Jen's discomfort, she and Ray left at the end of the school quarter for a visit with his family in Hong Kong. They will return to Seattle in time to unpack and meet us at the airport. Whew. Somebody inherited her mother's tendency to overcommit!

Speaking of Edith, she explored yet another employment option this year: Tennis Club Custodian. Saddle Creek Sanitary Engineer. Captain Commode. Actually, she was the tennis club VP and agreed to the cleaning duties for a month so that the board could develop a job description. She ended up doing it for six months. That sudsy ammonia just gets in your veins, you know. Her more respectable profession continued to be planning Christian Education at church. She is grateful for this creative outlet and has been able to teach some adult classes as well as coordinate the children's program. In September, she became part of the paid (underpaid) staff at the church and took this as a sign that it was time to pass the custodial baton – her toilet brush – to another janitor.

Fudge 'R' Not Us. I guess Edith assumed it would be, since it's 'R' money, but her role so far is listener and interested observer of the purchases I make when she's gone for the day: FAX machine, chocolate warming tubs, PC w/modem (Ya gotta have that modem, I say. What the heck is a modem, she says.) Her anxiety in June over how we would do as a "team" was unnecessary. As she's watched me gearing up the business this fall, she sees that I'm very capable of making these decisions myself. Oh, she still does a little market research now and then, asking her tennis team whether we should add nuts, and should the label be black on gold or gold on black. I listen politely, but I've already figured it all out. I'm into production and accounts receivable and having a great time! Edith is amazed that I managed a thirty year career with IBM without her guidance.

As for sharing the house with Edie all day – that's going well. The frequent hugging whenever we pass in the living room is over (the retirees' honeymoon period) as is my preoccupation with organizing the house. Fine with Edith if I wanted to rearrange my stuff from the office, but:

> "Leave my box of paints and crayons on the pantry shelf alone. I am aware they've sat there unused for seven years, but I know where they are if I ever need them! And do all retired husbands go out and **buy** things every day?"

But we're finally settling in, having negotiated desks and office space and phone time (aaahh … at last….a second line).

Come January, Edith hopes to negotiate who cooks dinner, since my Christmas list includes a cooking program for my new computer. Really, it is a wonderful blessing to have this time together – an opportunity we never thought we'd have this soon. Now, Edith says, as soon as I get tired of playing with my software, we can leave the house and actually DO something. I don't personally think Edie will ever become part of the high-tech world. She says she might enroll in a computer course this winter along with a watercolor course she's been dying to take. A neat way to sort of balance her right and left brain. I don't know which side of her brain was working the other day when she came home, saw the answering machine blinking, picked up the phone and said, "Hello." (Oooohh, the lights are on but nobody's home.)

We had time for a few mini-vacations this year, particularly after my retirement. We started the fudge business in grand style with a trip to the Philadelphia Candy Show, stopping in Manassas on the way home to celebrate my sister's 50th birthday at her favorite Chinese restaurant. It was a raucous affair fueled by martinis and wine and abetted by her good friends and AT&T co-workers. We met Margaret's new beau finally – Kenny Robinson – a great guy who assured me of his affection for my sister during a break in the karaoke:

"Lishen, Tony; I *really* love your shisher."

Yeah, but will you love her in the morning?

Throw in a trip to the gorgeous beaches of Clearwater with the Rowlands in May, a visit to Keuka Lake for our periodic vacation with the Matthaidesses and a wedding at the Blocks, Cumberland Island with the Fords, the installation of our former priest, Sam Candler, as Dean of the Cathedral in Columbia, SC, and a few retreats for Edith and we'd have to say it's been a FULL year. Thanks be to God.

We send you all our love and prayers,

P. S. Weren't these letters supposed to get shorter when the children left home? Wait til the grandchildren come.

The Cobourns
110 Canter Court
Roswell, GA 30076-1013
Christmas, 1994

Merry Christmas,

1994!! A glorious year filled with new beginnings and new life for us!

The first beginning: a grandson – Christopher – born to Jen and Ray in Seattle on May 22. Jen, Ray, and Edith thought they had contrived a great plan for this event. The parents and Baby Tse would spend the first five to seven days together, bonding in their 90's kind of way. Then Grammy would fly in to relieve and assist. Christopher was born on Sunday. Jennifer went home on Monday. (Within a few years, they'll be doing this on an outpatient basis, I predict.) On Monday night, Ray called:

> (plaintively) "Edith, do you have your bags packed yet?"
>
> "No – not really, Ray, since I'm not coming 'til Saturday. Remember?"
>
> "Well, we were wondering if you might like to come sooner ... like tomorrow."

Ah, it's wonderful to be needed – and wonderful to have a son-in-law honest enough to ask for help. So out she went to meet our sweet, gorgeous, precious new Christopher. Edith's memories of her own mother's visit at Jennifer's birth were unpleasant and they had begun to gnaw at her as Jen's due date grew closer. But God brought some healing for Edith through this event. It was a very fulfilling two weeks for her.

Believe it or not, this is the 21st edition of this letter. We are now making it available in large type for the visually challenged (which apparently includes an increasing number of our correspondents as we continue to get many of your rebuttals addressed to ZIP 30075 instead of 30076). Let's get it right, people!

Anyway, the old Fudgemeister has been stirring up a lot more than just memories this year, believe you me. Ever the opportunistic entrepreneur, I have built my business on one of the four basic food groups – which, as you know, are fudge, veggies, pepperoni pizza, and light beer. I have been cooking chocolate and maple walnut and butterscotch and peanut butter swirl and honey raisin for real customers this year. Ah, gossamer dreams of solvency. My income was double that of last year and my net losses were a third of 1993's. At this rate, by the millennium I'll be in the black. I hope so. If Newt Gingrich revives orphanages, can debtor's prison be far behind?

My endocrinologist thinks it is ironic that a diabetic makes fudge for a living. Sampling was one of several things he scolded me about this spring after a little flare-up of symptoms. So I stopped being a bad boy, lost 25 pounds, and agreed to attend a diabetic education course – along with my personal support group: Edith Cobourn. Of course, Edith doesn't just sit quietly at these classes. She is a full participant – like a diabetic wannabe. As the dietician discussed exercise and heart rates, we were all asked to take our own pulse, then report our rate per ten seconds to the instructor.

Tony? Eleven. Mr. Hanson? Thirteen. Carmen? Twelve. Edith? Seven. "Well," the instructor gently responded, "Most rates are between 10 and 12. Let's use 10 for you, Edith." Edith later admitted she couldn't find her pulse at all, so she made one up. I asked her why she had made up such a low number. "Because I wanted to have the best heartbeat," she said. She's lucky they didn't strap on the paddles and yell, "Clear!"

Andy is still at The Point in the heart of Atlanta's Wha's Happenin' neighborhood – cooking, tending bar, prepping – singing a little around town, and writing a little in his new warehouse apartment (is that an oxymoron?). The new digs, which he shares with two other guys, are right downtown. I mean <u>right</u> downtown. The bail bondsman and detention center are closer than the grocery store. If they still played baseball, you could hear the Braves game without a radio. Of course, this move did not worry Edith at all. ("Are you sure you'll be all right, honey?") In reality, with all the cops cruising in and out of the nearby lockups, it's probably safer than downtown Mayberry. Andy's current transportation to and from work, at 6 PM and 4 AM, respectively, is his new Cannondale mountain bike. This situation does not worry Edith either.

"Do you wear a helmet, honey? Does your bike have lights?"

"Actually, Mom, in the neighborhoods I ride through, I'd rather they didn't know I was approaching."

We were puzzled as to why Andy didn't get his car fixed this summer. Turns out it was a choice between auto repairs and an airline ticket to Vail to ski for a week with his main squeeze, Suzanne. Anyway, we had a chance to meet the new romantic interest when she joined us for Thanksgiving dinner. Suzanne is a lovely girl and we enjoyed her company very much.

Liz became Elizabeth when she moved to Seattle last year. To us, she is still Liz or Lizzie or Lizard. She matures as we regress. Seattle, lovely city that it is, has attracted several visitors to Elizabeth's quarters. One, a friend from college, encouraged her to apply to a summer camp he's worked at for several years. Liz thought about that for a minute and sent in her application. Bam. Done. And as visions of backpacking danced in her head, she was off to Maine to teach crafts and ropes courses and dine from a kosher menu. Ooooops! Joel forgot to mention that it was a Jewish camp. No problem. Liz became a vegetarian. So, between a no fat diet and the great outdoors, she'd gotten pretty svelte by the time she stopped in Atlanta on her way home.

Liz is a biker, too. That word has a different connotation these days, although Liz does now have a tattoo: a small fish on her ankle. It started out to be a Christian symbol-looking fish, but turned out to be more of an angelfish. This way, depending on who's commenting about her tattoo, Liz can decide whether to evangelize or talk about guppies. We'll let you know how many converts she chalks up.

Her biking became serious for a while as she pursued a brief career as a courier. That lasted until she was grazed by a big blue van. She is now safely back serving at Chinooks, saving her money for school and for bridesmaid's duties at a friend's spring wedding back in Atlanta – obligations which, we are sad to say, will not allow her to be with us for Christmas.

After Christopher, the second most momentous new beginning for us this year was transferring to our new mission church. Enticed by an inspirational priest and a substantially reduced commute, we were immediately awed by the spirit and energy of this small parish whose congregation, by the way, has grown to more than 120 families in just a few months. My folk group alone has 19 members, more than most entire missions. We both feel blessed to have been called to this place. Could this be what the New Testament Church at Ephesus was like, Edith wonders, as she recalls her recent journey to the Holy Land?

She was in that neck of the woods in October for a two-week tour of Israel. We'd received a pleasant little surprise from the IRS refund guys and I gave Edie a different kind of Easter gift. I wanted to give thanks to God for what was probably the only time we'll ever get good news from the IRS. Anyway, I decided this journey would enrich her teaching ministry. She had dreamed of such a trip for so long and was truly overwhelmed. What an incredible experience she had – with wonderful leaders, a <u>great</u> roommate, and 20 fabulous folks in the tour. One highlight for her was a walk around the outside of the walls of old Jerusalem.

Her group had been warned never to go anywhere alone, especially at dark. Well … on a free afternoon, sitting in a park, looking toward the old city, she felt a strong call to the wall. (She was alone and it would soon be dark.) Off she went. From Mt. Zion down to the Kidron Valley, where she gazed over at Gethsemane and the Mount of Olives, and then back around took an hour and a half, walking briskly – especially through the Arab section of the city. (She was alone and it *was* dark and she was wearing shorts!) But she fulfilled a desire to walk where Jesus walked and to feel Him walking with her – a memory she will treasure always.

Well, in the immortal words of those great bluegrass philosophers Lester Flatt and Earl Scruggs, "I feel like the good things outweigh the bad." Actually, they said it that way, I think, just to get the meter right. The correct expression in the south is "I feel like *that* the good things outweigh the bad." There is a lesson in etymology here, ending with "Ah fale lahk 'at th' guhd thangs ahtway the bayud," and beginning with "I am persuaded that the positive elements in life far exceed the negative." Whatever.

Now that my fudge orders are almost filled, we are ready to decorate and catch the holiday spirit. After our 16-hour flight to the west coast last year,[1] we'll be glad to welcome Ray and Jen and Christopher from Seattle; Margaret and Kenny from Virginia; and Andy from the inner city for the holidays.

We send you our love and prayers,

---

[1] 'This could be a short story all by itself: Atlanta to Dallas. Two-hour layover. Dallas to Seattle. Unscheduled stop in Denver. Seattle fog-bound. Land in Portland. Three-hour delay while buses gathered for drive to Seattle. Arrive at 7 AM. Holiday spirit in the toilet!

The Cobourns
110 Canter Court
Roswell, GA 30076-1013
Christmas, 1995

Merry Christmas,

I thought 1995 was when the golden years were supposed to begin to glisten: IBM retiree starts cute little business that requires just ten hours a month but nets $150,000 a year, thus funding frequent European jaunts, not to mention a new Mercedes. Instead, the year began with the IBM retiree driving his old Honda to a variety of job network meetings to wring hands with other down-and-outers over man's inhumanity to man.

In reality, the cute little new business still flourishes – but mostly at Christmas. Ten hours a month yields something short of $150K; *plus* you have to suffer all the indignities of actually trying to *sell* the stuff! So, I traded those old indignities for new ones as I pounded the pavement, looking for a real job for the first time in 30 years. My worst fear was actually finding one. "Welcome, Mr. Cobourn. Now, here at Big Company, Inc., you get five days vacation the first year, plus one other optional day you may use any way you like!"

How generous. I think I'll use it today to go out and buy some lottery tickets and quit this stinking job. Luckily, they told me I was overqualified. "Overqualified" is an EEOC-avoidance way of saying, "You made too much money at IBM, Mr. Cobourn, to be happy here for very long. Besides, you're too old and when you have your stroke, our insurance rates will skyrocket. And I don't know *what* we'll do when you begin to drool on your keyboard." I was real close to a career opportunity with Kroger ("You want paper or plastic?").

Well........I got lucky. I was hired by the State of Georgia as a contract instructor teaching management classes to supervisors in companies new to Georgia. Yes, from corporate bureaucrat to government bureaucrat – your tax dollars at work. Actually, it's a very cost-effective program that incents companies to move to

Georgia without draining the state treasury with outrageous tax write-offs. And the neat thing for me is that it's almost full-time, but I can take off whenever I want. Plus, it pays for the Olympics tickets. I've taught supervisors who range from eager young Valujet employees; ("Gee, I didn't know you were allowed do *that*, Mr. Cobourn! Wow!") to crusty old General Motors curmudgeons; ("You can't teach ME anything, boy. Go ahead and try. And if I slip up momentarily and actually learn something, they won't let me use it back at the plant anyway.")

Jennifer and Ray are still in Seattle, although there was talk this year of a job opportunity for Ray in Saudi Arabia. Lions and tigers and bears, oh my! Jen, our 90's kind of gal, sends me a FAX to tell me she just sent me an e-mail, then calls to see if I got the FAX. This saves her time to manage Christopher, who is now 19 months old and <u>busy</u>! Jennifer has inherited her mother's reckless teaching skills. She teaches a Sunday school class of 5th grade girls, several of whom she overheard discussing which ones were wearing bras. Jen told them of her 5th grade experience when Rusty Butcher ran his hand down her back to discover that she was not yet wearing one. "Oh," he said, "We'll make you president of the I.B.T.C." (Itty Bitty Titty Committee) Needless to say, Jen and her students bonded instantly.

Liz has moved to McMenamin's Microbrewery and Pub, her current pre-nursing employer (yes, the pendulum has once again swung toward nursing). Edie went out to Seattle to help her find a car – a purchase which, we hope, will break her cycle of illnesses caused by walking to work in Seattle's rain. They were searching for VW bugs. Liz called about one ad she'd seen and reached a recent Asian émigré whose auto expertise exceeded her ability to express it. "Ees ma huhban car. He jus put in new crotch. You rike come over an drye eet?"

Liz has been accepted into a two-year nursing program at Seattle Community College, so she is gingerly balancing her savings program between the car and tuition. This is a difficult balancing act, particularly when "Ginger" pesters her frequently to splurge for another rock concert.

Andy has also changed employers, and now has a much more civil schedule as daytime bartender at the Stein Club on Peachtree

Street. The clientele is an upgrade too – fewer navel rings and heavy eye liner (this is on the guys) and more of your run-of-the-mill barflies, with an occasional homeless guy wandering in for a handout. The music career? He's in his third year of trying to become an overnight success. Tough business.

This spring, Edith went through some tough business, too, when, for budgetary reasons, her Christian Education job came to an end. Although she struggled mightily over this disappointment before surrendering it to the Lord, her sabbatical turned into a wonderful gift: her "roots" journey up north in the fall. She had heard just about enough of my family genealogies going back to Saxony. Since Edie was able to trace her family back only as far as her grandmother, it was time for action. She had lost a lot of her family history and memories when her parents both died in her 20's; and she still is not in touch with her sister, Martha.

Her first task was to find and display a picture of little Edith. She hadn't realized how carried away she had become until Andy, out for dinner with his new girlfriend, Shannon Montgomery, whispered, "Hey, Mom, what's with all the baby pictures?" She smiled and said, "Dad and I are enjoying little Edith." She's now up to Edith at 25, when her mother died. Whew! This is arduous work, but it brings healing and greater understanding.

The roots discovery included stops at some of her old homesteads and stomping grounds in Pittsburgh, Altoona, and Olean, NY, her mother's hometown. She was especially grateful for a visit with her cousin Eric, whom she had not seen in 40 years. Together, they reminisced through old neighborhoods about their rich childhood experiences with the Swedish clan. These strong Christians cherished their new life in America, and she remembered the joyful reunions and excellent cooking at the farm in Grassflat, Pa. Many of the aunts were professional cooks – one even cooked for the Mellons in Pittsburgh.

Edie remembers the adults on the porch gliders telling stories in Swedish so the little ones couldn't understand, and the wonderful simplicity of life then: being content to play all afternoon in Black Moshannon Creek (no waterslides), eating cucumbers straight from the garden (no Snackwell cookies in 16 flavors), running up and down the hills to the strip mines (no car pools to soccer leagues), stopping to pet the cows on the way home (no pedigreed pot-bellied pigs). Yes, life was good.

And life is still good! Despite her aborted Christian Ed. career, she did get to teach an adult education class: "How do we hear God's voice today;" or, as she taught it in her own throw-caution-to-the-wind style: "Construction paper for Christians." Think of a meaningful Bible verse and then make a tear art picture of it. When Edith teaches, she never knows if her class will follow instructions or go out and get a cup of coffee and whisper about her. Well, the tear art results were breathtakingly creative! I attended, of course, and, as the class clown, made a paper rib ("And God took a rib from Adam's side and made woman"). I wrote on the rib, "This is where girls come from." And Edith has been my "riblet" ever since. Just where she wants to be in God's kingdom.

We hope you're where you want to be in God's kingdom, and that you have a blessed Christmas and joyous New Year,

The Cobourns
110 Canter Court
Roswell, GA 30076-1013
Christmas, 1996

Merry Christmas,

Perhaps last year's plan for my peaceful semi-retirement was premature. I had finally reached that comfortable stage at which, when my Hamilton College magazine arrived, I read the necrology section first. A nap usually headed my list of one or two things to do. I upgraded my computer so Solitaire now runs *really* fast. Then, "STUFF" began to happen!

First, a new job for me. Good-bye Fudgemeister. Second, Edith got a job! Good-bye vacuuming. Third, Jen is pregnant with her second. Good-bye wine coolers. Fourth, Andy got engaged. Good-bye Andy. Fifth, Liz got engaged. Good-bye disposable income. Hello caterers.

My new job is still with QuickStart, but I am now a project manager, helping executives of new Georgia companies set up training plans for their newly hired employees. No more sporadic teaching assignments in East Lardbutt, Georgia. More stable income. Fewer naps.

Second, Edith is gainfully employed full-time (outside the home, we must add these days) for the first time since "Louie Louie" topped the charts. She skipped being a working mother and is now a working grandmother. Liberated after all these years of institutionalized marital oppression, she is Director of Christian Education for an Episcopal church in Dunwoody. After a year's sabbatical – stepping aside from her church work at our own parish, being quiet, and waiting....and waiting....to see what would come – that mighty wind blew in at the end of August. It whispered to her, "How would you like to go from three tennis teams to a real job?"

St. Martin in the Fields is 18 miles down the road, so she can now experience the bliss of the Atlanta commute. Once there, she finds a large and lively parish with three full-time clergy and a staff of six – a wonderful group to work with. She is responsible for teachers and programs for two-year olds through adults – "A snap," she thought to herself as she left the interview. Fear and trembling set in shortly, however, as she asked, "Lord, are you kidding me or what? Do you really think this is a good thing for me?"

Anyway, she now feels like Sarah – giving birth in old age. Sarah with Isaac; Edie with a job at 55. On her first day at work, I dutifully waved good-bye from the driveway – like a mommy seeing her first-born off to kindergarten. Shortly after getting to her office, she called home: "OK, I've put my office key on my key ring. Now what do I do?"

That state of innocence didn't last long. I remember Andy's line after starting his first job out of college: "Boy, I don't know how Dad has done this all these years. This takes up your whole day." Then she trudges home. When I'm in town, I cook dinner – an excellent reason for her to brighten up. On Tuesday, I do the laundry and on Friday, we clean the house together. This is about as good as it gets. However, she'd much rather do this than have a baby. (Thanks anyway, Sarah.)

Turns out the church staff does have a little fun occasionally. In fact, one day at work, they were just having a good time all day, and she said to one of the young assistant priests, "Kevin, do you ever feel guilty at the end of the day for having too much fun on the job?" He turned abruptly and, with a serious expression, asked, "Edith, have you read the New Testament?" Puzzled, she paused, then acknowledged that she had. Kevin's reply: "Grace! It's God's Grace, Edith." Yes, indeed.

Of course, this job situation has "given her permission to get in touch with her personhood," which means, among many other things, dragging me to every relational movie in town. I used to love 19th century England – the dark moors, the thatched roofs, the push-'em-up bosoms – but Jane Austen's dialogue is killing me!

Tony: Yo! Edith. You want some coffee?

Edith: Oh, my very dear Mr. Cobourn, you have been ever so kind to me for such an exquisitely long time. Dare I presume to impose on your graciousness again just this once?

Tony: Leaded or unleaded?

Putting this obvious talent for dialogue to work, I am volunteering as a reader for the blind at a local radio station which broadcasts throughout the state – the Georgia Radio Reading Service (GaRRS). Andy's fiancée, who is also a reader there, pointed out this opportunity. So far, I have not read any Jane Austen. Not even Dr. Seuss. They started me off with the Waycross Journal-Herald.

I read stuff like this:

> Caption: "Meet Satilla Regional's Physical Therapy Team"
>
> Headline: "Police Roundup – Burglary: Canned Goods, Eggs, Beer, and Jewelry Taken From a Samuel Street Home on Monday.
>
> News Article: "' ... With this program,' Powell said, 'we will be able to provide each child with two worm treatments a year ... '"
>
> Column: " ... The Octoberfest was enjoyed by many at the Ware Nursing Home. The gala included entertainment by both the Georgia Line Dancers and the Victorious Believers ... "

Yee haw!

I also read the obituaries, but not the TV listings (ha ha). Clearly, GaRRS has yet to fully appreciate my talent.

OK, third – Jen is pregnant again. Her baby is due in June, a pivotal date for the fourth and fifth events – the upcoming weddings. So, who could be cuter and more brilliant than your first grandchild? Undoubtedly your second. Meanwhile, Jen and Ray supply us with Fritopher stories. Fritopher, is, of course, Christopher, just as Bampy is Grampy. (See reference above to Bampy's talent for dialogue. The kid is equally articulate.) For example, Ray bonds with Fritopher at Burger King. Recently, the boy beat the father rolling the window down and ordering "hamberder, phies, techup....pease?.....otay?" We're going to Seattle for Christmas to check out the Junk Food King and his prince.

Fourth, Andy is engaged to a sweet and delightful girl, Shannon Montgomery, whom he met last year. We could not be happier with this match. They will be married October 4th in the chapel of Atlanta's Episcopal Cathedral. Andy, who has inherited his father's flair for romance and drama, proposed to her on a Florida beach the night before her brother's wedding, just as a shooting star arced across the sky. Shannon's wish was that they could be married some day, at which point Andy pulled out the ring and fell to one knee. Shannon, too stunned to say, "What took you so long?" simply responded, "Yes."

And fifth, Liz is engaged to Jason Joss, a co-worker from McMenamin's in Seattle. We don't know him very well, and I reminded Jason of that when he called us to ask for Liz's hand – a reminder which stopped his heart momentarily. It started beating again when I said he had come highly recommended by both Liz and Jennifer, and we would be very pleased to have him as a son-in-law. They were with us for Thanksgiving, so we got to approve first hand. Liz and Jen were right. He's a charming guy and loves Liz very much. They think the wedding will be August 3rd, in Washington State, perhaps at a resort on one of the San Juan islands. We have known for some time that we were blessed with three wonderful children. Now we are thankful to have been blessed with three wonderful children-in-law.

Liz has the time, unfortunately, to plan for the wedding since her on again, off again nursing quest is off again. Accepted last year into Seattle Community College's RN program, she was notified that the course had been cancelled for 1996 and she would be re-enrolled for the class beginning in 1997! The volatilility of the health care industry has struck the ranks of nurses. Nationwide, facilities are cutting staff due to budget pressures. Last year, since *none* of the Seattle CC grads found a job, the school chose not to add to the glut. When, oh when will Liz realize her dream? This is starting to feel like a biblical plague.

Well, the Olympics were Exciting! Exhausting! And, in the end, Over! We had a brief panic attack after our mortgage-sized ticket order, but we were over it by the time the seats were confirmed – an excellent variety of events, including opening ceremonies, volleyball, and rowing. We had two shifts here – the Matthaidesses the first week and a houseful of Cobourn kids the second. By the way, just in case you are not yet convinced that worldwide communications are instantaneous, Ray got a call from his mother in Hong Kong a few minutes after the Centennial Park bombing. She was watching CNN and wondered if we had been at the park and if we were OK.

But don't believe all the negative junk that has been written about Atlanta's traffic and safety and commercialism. It was a glorious adventure – from the claustrophobic two hours it took to get through security at the opening ceremonies, to the frustration of trying to watch five gymnastics events simultaneously, to the thrill of seeing Gail Devers explode through the third leg of the women's 4X100 relay final crushing Jamaica, to the two drunken Swedes Edith attracted for a photo opportunity at the Olympic Stadium. Ya sure. You betcha. A glorious adventure, indeed.

Of course, the Olympic spirit didn't necessarily spill over into all the surrounding communities. Cordele's huge billboard on I-75 "welcomed the world" to its annual watermelon festival from July 19-21. The world forgot to come. And the folks in Metter ("Everything's Better in Metter") were sorely disappointed when no one came to see the five giant tractor tires they had painted in the colors of the Olympic rings. Here in Roswell, the city fathers spent a gazillion dollars to underwrite a historical festival during the games. A gazillion dollar bomb. Why would people drive 30 miles to see the Roswell High Flag Corps when they came to Atlanta to watch Michael Johnson?

Oh, well. So went 1996. Lots of joy, some disappointment, a little grace.

We hope you experienced some of God's grace this year, too. Have a wonderful holiday season,

The Cobourns
110 Canter Court
Roswell, GA 30076-1013
Christmas, 1997

Merry Christmas,

This will be our first Christmas without any of our kids coming home. We know it will be quiet, but we're not certain silence and a snail's pace is necessarily a good tradeoff for family hugs and harmonizing on the Doxology before Christmas dinner.

This new state of affairs is the direct result of the "stuff" I wrote about last year. Liz and Jason Joss were married on August 3rd at Rosario Resort on Orcas Island, in the San Juan Islands north of Seattle. It was an outdoor ceremony, held on a bluff overlooking Puget Sound. God blessed us with a most beautiful day and provided a breathtaking setting with the islands in the background and majestic sailboats promenading up the sound. Harp and trumpet and song ushered in the wedding party. An inspirational homily from Bill Harper, a wonderful young priest flown in from Bainbridge Island, brought tears of joy from the congregation and a smile of victory from Liz.

The Josses are northwest natives. They are a large, fun-loving, close-knit family, and we all got along very well and very quickly. Of course, given the trek to get to the wedding site (90 minute drive north from Seattle, one hour wait for a ferry, 90 minute ferry ride to Orcas, 20 minute drive to Rosario), we probably would have blended well with Charles Manson's family by the time we arrived.

Since everyone was from "out of town," everyone attended the rehearsal dinner, providing a raucous audience for the traditional Cobourn musical tribute to the bride and groom. This time I wrote some lyrics to John Denver's "Back Home Again" and Andy and I presented it to Liz and Jason.

There was a small but high-quality contingent from the east coast. The majority in attendance, however, were Josses plus every living Sigma Nu alumnus from the University of Oregon. (Just to give you a flavor for how the reception *might* have turned out,

Jason's fraternity was the one at which "Animal House" was filmed.) The evening reception was calm, though, and was highlighted by the cutting of a funky, day-glo wedding cake, with the barefoot bride and her groom shmushing it in each other's faces, as is the custom these days.

Jason continues his work as a manager at McMenamin's, but Liz has "retired." Now, after several false starts over the years, she is enrolled in nursing school. Be still my heart! This is an incredible answer to a lifelong dream of hers – ever since, at age seven, she told her grandmother she "wanted to be a nurse so she could see all the naked bodies."

Barely two months later, we gathered again for Andy's marriage to Shannon Montgomery, held on October 4, in the beautiful chapel of the Episcopal Cathedral in Atlanta. Their priest, a colleague of Edith's at St. Martin's, came to be their friend over the course of the year's planning. During Kevin's homily, he referred to the embarrassing stories friends and family had told about the bride and groom at the rehearsal dinner the evening before. The tales reminded him of the Genesis passage: *"That* is why a man leaves his father and mother and is united with his wife."

The reception was at Houston Mill House. It's a charming old house near Emory University with spacious grounds and lots of gathering rooms. The Cobourn Family Singers did their swan song – a final performance dedicated to a marrying sibling. This time it was Harry Chapin's "Story of a Life." If you know Andy, play it sometime. We all got chills. We have pictures of Andy and Shannon getting chills from our rendition. Since Andy, my principal accompanist, was otherwise occupied, I had to put together a new band. I enlisted one of Andy's buddies on guitar; I sang lead; Edie, Jen, and Liz were backup. I called them my Honky Supremes. Real tight harmonies.

Once again we've lucked into a great family-in-law. Shannon's parents are very gracious. And they are now our closest living relatives since Andy and Shannon, with all their belongings in a 24' Ryder truck, headed for a fresh start in Seattle. <u>What IS the attraction out there?</u>

A wedding footnote: As many of you know, bridal registration is no longer limited to china and silver. One actually walks around a store with a laser scanning wand and a hand-held PC and creates the ultimate wish list. Our kids registered at Crate and Barrel for pots and pans and oven mitts, Home Depot for smoke alarms and duct tape, Safeway for frozen corn and a case of Bass Ale, and Pizza Hut for their next meal.

Jen and Ray deserve Mother- and Father-of-the-Year Awards for their participation in two out of town family weddings while managing both a toddler and an infant. Yes, we predicted last year that a new baby would arrive in June and we were right! Anna Elizabeth Tse (Ray suggested the middle name and it was a surprise to Liz) was born on June 9. She is healthy and beautiful. Two kids, one of each, and that's enough, says Jennifer.

Christopher, now 3 1/2, is in pre-school a few days a week so Jen can get a life. Two former comedians run the school. (I am not making this up!) These two owners apparently did the west coast version of the borscht belt for a few years. I think it's called the látte loop in Seattle. They then decided to go into a closely related field: day care. It is sort of like a Stiller and Meara head start program. Christopher loves it. After only his first day he came home and said, "Mom, did you hear the one about the pastor, the priest, and the rabbi?" Jen started laughing and Anna started crying. Christopher snapped right back with, "Take my sister — PLEASE!" (OK, I *did* just make that up.)

As for me, I continue to toil part time for the state, teaching and developing orientation programs for companies moving to Georgia. I've joined the board of a friend's foundation, owner of several nursing homes around the country. We make periodic visits to the homes, monitoring costs, staffing, etc. Having seen the nursing home industry from a client's view when my mother lived in one for eight years, this different perspective is fascinating. Larry's facilities are fastidiously maintained by very caring staffs, and this sideline offers me just enough diversion, travel and new knowledge to round out my semi-retired life. My friends now tell me nursing home jokes, none of which is appropriate for a Christmas letter. They think I'm hilarious at the homes, though.

I tell the same jokes on each visit, which they've forgotten since the last time.

For Edith, this was a stressful and emotional year as she grew in her job and married off her kids. She was "Home Alone" after "Two Weddings and a Grandbaby" while working "9 to 5." It felt like a year-long Outward Bound experience, she says. Raising three kids was easier than 1997. After all, she acquired them one at a time over six years – a gradual adaptation to her first job: motherhood. So, "Hello, Edith! Welcome to the working world!" The scales have fallen from her eyes, and her hat is off to all of you who have done this forever. She wonders if this gets easier.

Her job at St. Martin's has required more personal growth than she sometimes felt necessary, and she entered some of those growth spurts kicking and screaming. She told me she has often felt like sweet Anna, struggling in the birth canal. It is indeed a painful process to be born into a new vocation. Anyway, after one year and three months, she is thankful to see some redemption and comfort.

Well, we miss our wonderful kids and grandkids this season but, at the same time, we are pleased they have each other's company in Seattle. It is time for Edie and me to be alone – after 33 years of raising and launching a family. And so we wait this Advent season, preparing for God's coming again, and wonder just what that will mean for each of us……………..

Sending you our love and prayers,

The Cobourns
110 Canter Court
Roswell, GA 30076-1013
Christmas, 1998

Happy Holidays,

We remember the chaos that was 1997 in pastels now, with the poignant nudging aside the terrifying. Edith and I have only each other to annoy these days. This is our first full year without any children nearby, and it's a difficult transition from 34 years of child nurturing and butt kicking. Surely this is a test and someone will tell us soon whether we've passed. One conclusion I think we're coming to was expressed so well by that wise poet, Ricky Nelson, in his *Garden Party*: "Can't please everyone, so you got to please yourself."

Part of this year's test focused on the employment market. I had thought that, as we approach sixty, there need not be an "employment market." But, whether to fulfill ourselves or to pay the cable bill on time, there we were. Edith left her job at St. Martin's in the summer, frustrated by a lack of clergy support there for Christian Education. She agonized over the decision for months – like Jacob wrestling with the Lord ("I will not let you go until you have blessed me.") Finally, she realized she received her blessings from her teachers and program leaders, not from the hierarchy, and she was able to move on. She concluded that she was the transition from the 18-year regime of her predecessor to whatever the next phase was to be for Christian Ed. at St. Martin's. She left the job exhausted, but pleased that it took two people to replace her.

Edie is now working part-time as the assistant to our Rector at St. Aidan's in Alpharetta. Her "recovery from life in general" is progressing. A few weeks ago, she discussed life with a friend:

> EDIE: "I don't know; lately I just feel......kind of......oh.......fuzzy-brained."
> PEGGY: "Well, give me an example of what you mean."
> EDIE: "Oh, I just.....um.......I don't......."

PEGGY: "Just any incident that comes to your mind."

EDIE: "Well, what exactly do you mean by 'fuzzy-brained'?"

PEGGY: (Pause.) "I don't know. That was *your* word, Edith."

EDIE: "Oh."

My employment change was slightly less traumatic. I started working part-time for Larry Butler, whose foundation owns six nursing homes. Just Larry and me and a secretary who moves her lips when she reads. I'm doing Human Resources stuff for those facilities and have traded driving around Georgia with QuickStart for flying around the Midwest. I do not miss the Atlanta drivers (motto: Start late. Drive fast. Finger in ready position at all times). Flights to Michigan City, Indiana, have their own charm, of course (teeny planes, late at night, dead of winter). Plus, you get captivating conversation from seatmates on overbooked flights. For example: Dapper Old Guy (DOG) plops himself down next to me on the inevitably late and full flight out of Cincinnati:

DOG: "I am a man of substantial means, but I refuse to fly First Class. I just *hate* that name, don't you? First Class!"

ME: "Mmmm."

DOG: "I mean, as if we should have *classes* in America. Honestly! My father was chairman of this airline, and we had some great battles over this issue, believe you me. So.....where are you going?"

ME: "Well, I'm uh ... "

DOG: "Me, I'm heading for my winter place in Florida – got another leg after this one. Of course, my limo will pick me up in Gainesville. I own a chain of banks down there."

ME:

DOG: "Hey, how about that market, huh? I left $250,000 in with one broker and after all the ups and downs I made seven bucks. Huh? Amazing, huh?

Hey, I heard somebody a couple rows up mention
pizza. I own a chain of pizza shops in Chicago...."

I knew him so well when we landed in Atlanta that it seemed unnecessary to exchange business cards.

The three kids are still hanging out on the left coast, although Jen and Ray moved a couple of states south, to L.A. Ray took a job with Disney. He is Pluto on weekends and holidays. (No, I made that up.) He is one of Disney's sourcing managers and finds Asian manufacturers for the products sold at Disney World and the Disney stores. Jennifer has found the relocation process as uplifting as Edith and I did at her age. They're living in Sierra Madre which, Jen says, has the same small-town feel that her Seattle neighborhood had. But everybody misses Uncle Andy, Aunt Shannon, Uncle Jason, and Aunt Liz. They'll all be together in Seattle for Christmas.

Andy's selling pools and spas and playing golf whenever he can. Shannon just took a new job as Assistant Director of Admissions for the Seattle Art Institute. They're becoming acclimated to Seattle, but still miss Atlanta. We were thrilled to have them with us for Thanksgiving. Jason's proving to be a key asset to McMenamin's, and Liz is one semester away from her nursing degree. We'll visit Seattle in June for Liz's graduation. Party on. Life's a struggle when you're young – a fact that numbs you nicely for the time you discover that life's a struggle when you're old.

Have a blessed Christmas and a joyous New Year,

The Cobourns
110 Canter Court
Roswell, GA 30076-1013
Christmas, 1999

Merry Christmas and Happy New Millennium,

First, a note about last year's abbreviated letter. Edie said there wasn't ONE DAMN THING FUNNY about 1998. I'll tell you more about that later but, rest assured, life improved significantly in 1999.

When I changed jobs last year, my friend's foundation owned six nursing homes, primarily in the Midwest. My HR job and the management training I do are great fun – part-time, independent, working with outstanding people! Every semi-retired guy should be this lucky. But Larry now owns 30 homes and we're still growing, both numerically and geographically, so I've been slowly increasing my hours. Now ... some longstanding recipients of this letter may be tempted to suck up to me for preferential room selection in Boston, Indianapolis, Tyler, etc. Control yourselves; particularly those of you who are already shuffling around in warm-up pants and drooling uncontrollably. Our standards are very high.

Edie's birthday present to me last year was a two-day class at Emory University on writing for publication. I had long considered publishing these letters and the class was just the push I needed to get serious before I got dead. The instructor hooked me up with an editing group: three pastors and me. I was grateful we were editing my Christmas letters instead of some of my other literary efforts in which the language is more colorful. Three of the group were terrific. We eased out the fourth participant – a retired minister who had served as a chaplain in Viet Nam and has since viewed everything in life through a haze of Agent Orange. Instead of suggesting grammatical changes or improvements in literary clarity, he moralized to us about how we *should* have felt while writing a particular vignette. We needed an editor, not a spiritual director.

The group said that, for publication, the letters must be in one voice – not the joint Edie and Tony effort you've been receiving. So,

I've been revising all the old letters and the process has been both fascinating and nostalgic. I've discovered, however, that I'm missing a couple of years (1976 and 1994). If any of you compulsive savers have these, I'd appreciate copies. Otherwise, I'll have to make things up. I'll keep you posted on the publishing venture. If it happens, I'll need releases from those of you I've maligned over the years.

Our kids remain far away. Jen and Ray are still in Sierra Madre – near Pasadena. They love their little home town and are rediscovering sunshine and backyards. Christopher started kindergarten this year and is doing well. Anna is two, and you know the rest of *that* story. When she started talking, we were Weemy and Weepy. Now she can say Gammy and Grampy. (Gosh, they grow up so fast, don't they?) For Christmas, I'm giving her a t-shirt that says, **"WARNING! I'M TWO!"** Christopher, at five, loves to talk on the phone. (His mother doesn't know this but he even called us at Liz's in Seattle during our June visit.) One day, preoccupied at play, he came in from the back yard to say hello on the phone to Grammy.

"Hi, Christopher!"

"Hi, Grammy."

"I miss you, Christopher."

"I miss you too, Grammy ... (pause) ... Um, I just
started missing you."

Andy and Shannon are still in Seattle. Andy has returned to school full time at the Seattle Art Institute for a degree in mixed media/graphics/audio technology. He is excited about this new direction and is really enjoying the artistic challenges of the field. His dedication level has risen a bit, too, from his lead-guitar days at UGA. Funny how little things like marriage, rent, cars, and food reprioritize your life. Work and school schedules often conflict, so Shannon says that, for the next year and a half, their conversation will be limited to one intense 10-minute period a day.

The school, and Andy's part-time evening job, are in the area where anarchists recently "protested" the World Trade Organization meeting. Andy had to register on the morning of the second day (when the curfew was declared and a fifty-square block cordoned off). He had no problem. But the area schools and businesses shut down for several days so Andy and Shannon had an unexpected vacation.

The big news from Liz and Jason came on October 14th with the birth of Samuel Cobourn Joss, a hefty and brilliant child who looks just like me (my sister says). Jason's brother, Brad, a northwest techie, took a bunch of digital pictures within a few hours of the birth, went home and created a web page for Sam, beaming the news to Oregon, Australia, Washington, D.C., Hong Kong, and many points in between. What an unbelievable age these kids are being born into!

<u>Liz graduated from nursing school in June</u> and both the Cobourn and Joss clans gathered for that huge event. Some of you may remember that this quest began more than ten years ago. She's wanted to be a nurse forever, but her high school record was not strong. After two years at Young Harris College in the north Georgia mountains, she was diagnosed with an auditory processing deficit. Brenau College in Gainesville offered some special help for ADD-related problems and Liz did very well academically. She did not care for the all-girl environment, though. What followed was a series of applications to, and rejections from, a variety of local and state nursing programs. Finally she moved to Seattle and was accepted at Seattle Community College. It has been a struggle, but we're <u>very</u> proud of her! (Modesty prevents me from telling you her GPA – let's just say it was higher than 3.66.)

Well, while I've continued to breadwin, Edith has been in recovery – from life in general and 1997 in particular. She's just taken her medicine, so I can tell you all about it without fear of retribution:

Our Christmas letter for 1997 was deceptively joyful. Two weddings, a full-time job, Anna's birth in Seattle, surgery for Edith, and, with Andy's departure, the last of our kids to move west ... all of that put her over the edge. The result? Depression.

Since she'd never experienced this before, it took a long time to figure out, so dark clouds have covered her last two years. "Let the land lie fallow after bearing much fruit" were the words she heard after leaving the Christian Ed. Job at St. Martin's in '98. Good advice which, of course, she ignored, jumping right back into a part-time Christian Ed. position at our home parish.

She finally heeded the message this summer, and is taking the time to rest, refuel, and find her place again. She traded the authority, prestige, and money for an improved emotional state. After a year of therapy, she has identified all her life's issues. (Oh, was *that* a joyous exercise!) And then, of course, there's the anti-depressant medication. Whoooeee! You GO, girl! She sends hugs and kisses and heartfelt thanks to her friends and family members who walked through this with her. Me – I tiptoed through this with her. When you ask your wife how she is in the morning and she replies, "I don't *know* yet. How come you keep <u>asking</u> me that?" that's the time to tiptoe.

During her break from job responsibilities, she is tackling some major redecorating projects, e.g. the whole house. She says it's time for some neglected parts of her life. Relocating used to solve this problem for her. Her mother always put the same furniture in the next house and remade the curtains to fit the new windows. Edie emulated her for a long time, but we've been here 18 years now. When the pest control guy goes into the dining room and says, "Wow, I haven't seen rust-colored shag in a long while," you know it's time for a change.

I guess some of her recovery actually began before she said "Yes!" to drugs. Last year she was involved in a study on centering prayer – a very quiet, reflective process. Since depression shuts you down anyway, it was a great fit. And her spiritual director encouraged her to practice twice a week as a start, not twice a day. Her motto is, "Aim low!" Edie loves the counter-culture sound of that, having recently exited the go-go-go workplace. The director's advice sounds like the objective I set for my athletically challenged tennis team: "Set easy goals, then fail to achieve them." Edie's current therapy includes lots of tennis, and her current prayer is for God to help her take things more seriously – especially laughter, parties, and dancing.

I think her prayer ought to include a plea for relief from automobile trauma. This year's incidents began with her visit to Becky Jordan, Jen's college buddy. Edie's car was parked in Becky's driveway when Becky backed out of her garage and totaled Edie's car. (Not Edith's fault, but remember, Edith is a facilitator.) Then she got a parking ticket. (She parked in a police parking space at a police station.) Then she got a traffic ticket. (She made a left turn through a red light, and the cop *who was right behind her* pulled her over.) Finally, a cement post at the drive-through ATM she was *backing out of* jumped out and bit off her rear bumper. Well, her car got so it was afraid to go to the grocery store. Edie, by now familiar with a variety of emotional distresses, bought the old Jetta some new tires, changed her oil, and dropped a couple of Prozacs into her gas tank. Everything's fine.

Edie's studies this year could be entitled "West Meets East." She is intrigued with the wisdom of the Eastern religions. Her group has read books by a Hindu meditation teacher, a Buddhist nun, and a Christian who combines centering prayer and Tai Chi. She's currently studying with a Presbyterian Zen teacher. So she is ready now, no matter who has the one and only true God. At the end of the meditation, they bow in the Japanese style to acknowledge the goodness in each other. Edie thinks that's wonderful. She says she is tired of looking at the sinner in herself and wants to concentrate on the positive elements. Do I hear an "Amen?"

Blessings to you this holiday season,

The Cobourns
110 Canter Court
Roswell, GA 30076-1013
Christmas, 2000

Merry Christmas and Happy New Millennium,

The salutation, same as last year's, is for the purists who know that *this* January 1st is the beginning of the new century, not last January 1st. If the millennium bug prevents you from receiving this letter, call us at our bunker and we'll have the militia deliver you another copy.

We spent last Christmas in L.A. with Jen, Ray, and the kids. There is *nothing* like sharing a Christmas morning with grandchildren, although it's still a little strange to look out the back window and see sun shining on orange trees.

Later in the week, Ray, Christopher, and I were resting at Starbuck's after a morning walk. Christopher led the conversation:

> Christopher: "How come your throat hangs down, Grampy?"
> Ray: "Christopher!! Don't ask........."
> Christopher: "His neck is kind of fluffy."
> Ray: "CHRISTOPHER!"
> Me: "It's because Grampy is really a big turkey. Gobblegobblegobblegobble."
> Christopher: "Hahahahahahahahaha."

Christopher is obviously a keen observer of the human condition. For some reason I am typically the observee. On the way to the airport last year, Christopher, from the back seat, and to no one in particular, said, "Hmmm, Grampy seems a little bald." ("CHRISTOPHER!" his mother screamed) "And he seems a little bit pudgy, too." By this time Edith and Jennifer were holding their sides laughing. I think their response sends the wrong message to six year olds, in whom one should try to develop a more profound sense of dignity and respect.

Edith's classes this year migrated from the spiritual to the pragmatic. She took a "55 Alive" Senior Citizens driving class in which a very old person read them the Georgia Driver's Manual for four hours each day. Picture Tim Conway shuffling up to the podium. In the spring she took an art class taught by a cute, clueless young thing. Edie assumes she's a Theta from the University of Georgia. (Do you readers of the coed persuasion know what that means?) In the first ten minutes of the first two hour class, the instructor described the supplies they'd need.

> "Would you like to go out and buy them now?" she said.
> "No," they replied, "We have an hour and fifty minutes left of the class we just paid for."
> "OK," she said. "Take off your shoe and draw it."
> In the next class the teacher instructed them to draw an apple.
> "Hey," said one outspoken senior citizen, "Are you going to **teach** us how to draw something? I can sit home and do *this*!"

On Wednesdays, Edie goes to line dancing class, vowing never again to sit on the sidelines while the rest of the wedding guests do the shag. Watch TNN for a few minutes and you'll see what she looks like. Thursday is her Microsoft Word class. At night, she knocks me off the computer while she practices selecting and pasting and saving.

Meanwhile, back in Los Angeles, Ray left Disney in January to take a job in Chicago as the COO of a company called The Product Zone, a division of Havi, the outfit which supplies McDonalds. His company is responsible for providing McDonald's with all its games and giveaway products. Jennifer and the kids stayed in Sierra Madre until the end of the school year to see how the boy from Hong Kong survived a Windy City winter. He handled the weather, but found an even better job opportunity in the spring with a competitor based in Hong Kong, whose U.S. headquarters was in Dallas. Ray has since taken over their U.S. operation and moved the office to Los Angeles. Now *there's* a novel way to avoid a relocation.

Liz's baby, Sam, was baptized in April at Bill Harper's church on Bainbridge Island. Bill is the priest who married Liz and Jason in 1997. (Remember the description of the ceremony? Liz with her ankle tattoo and Bill with his earring?) Seattle remains the place to go if you want to adopt an alternative lifestyle. As we lingered over the obligatory látte and scones after the ferry ride to Bainbridge, I browsed the signs in the window of the establishment next door: The Glass Onion and TapeWorks Store. They advertised an upcoming ultimate Frisbee competition, foot/hand massages at Thursday's Reflexology class (bring your own pillow, towel, lotion, and colored pen), and a West African drum and dance class on Wednesday evening (drums are provided ; bring your own West African, I guess).

In May, Edie and I attended our first Cobourn family reunion. We met in Albuquerque, home to Mary Jane (my father's last remaining sibling) and two of her children. Seven of the nine cousins made it for an extended weekend of sharing family stories and old pictures of Uncle Elmer and Aunt Gerty, et al. Funny how important roots are becoming to me lately. Sadly, our kids don't have cousins, and we hope their children stay in touch with each other. Edie and I did not keep up with ours and we are the poorer for it.

Let's see ... the Seattle contingent is flourishing. Jason loves his new job with Catalyst Marketing, a company that provides promotional items to businesses. Sam now has teeth and is walking. (I wonder if I'll be able to say the same thing about myself in a few years.) Liz, having passed her nursing boards, is interviewing for part-time work at a local hospital. In the spring, she took up triathlons and Shannon joined her in one this summer. Brother, I needed to put a glycerin tablet under my tongue just to write about that! Shannon's still recruiting for the Art Institute of Seattle, where Andy has two quarters left for his degree in mixed media. He's already preparing for the job market, developing a portfolio and doing some free-lance website design.

In October, Edith surprised me for my 60th birthday by having Jen, Andy, and Liz fly to Atlanta for the weekend. She asked me what I wanted most for this important milestone. I said I'd really like to have the kids come home – and we chuckled about the impracticality of that and how we had just been to L.A. for Labor Day weekend.... Well, the week before my birthday, Edie decided to go for it. She called all three on Wednesday night, asked them if they could get away and, incredibly, by Thursday evening, all reservations were made, baby-sitters arranged, and they were set to come home – all with their spouses' blessings.

The intervening week almost did Edie in. She was sick with the flu and struggling hard to maintain the conspiracy. Liz and Andy were arriving Wednesday morning on the red-eye from Seattle. How would they get up to Roswell? What would they do all day? Could she find them a place to sleep? Who would pick up Jennifer that afternoon? What if I came home early that day?

She had used my frequent flier points for Andy's ticket and Delta sent the itinerary to me. Edie, by this time delirious from illness and intrigue, forgot to intercept the mail. But only part of the jig was up. I showed her the itinerary and she melted into tears. She was crying because the secret was unraveling, but she was clever enough to pretend that she was emotionally overcome by Andy's thoughtfullness. I still hadn't figured out that these were *my* frequent flier points because Delta had earlier mixed up my account with Andy's and I assumed they were at it again.

So, as we entered the restaurant for my birthday dinner, I was still practicing my reaction of stunned surprise at Andy's presence when, what to my wondering eyes should appear, all three of my children were having a beer! As you can imagine, the weekend was memorable. It was the first time just the five of us had been together since Jennifer moved to China in 1989. For all you younger Christmas correspondents out there, trying to decide what to do for the Old Farts on their birthday/anniversary/whatever, this is a much better idea than a raucous surprise party with cutsie gifts of Viagra and thong underwear.

As the year wound down, Jennifer and the kids spent Thanksgiving in Seattle. Edie and I got a call one night from Liz and Jen while Christopher, Anna, and Sam (six, three, and one) were destroying each other and Liz's living room. "Mom, we were wondering – how did you raise three children all by yourself?" This triggered Edie's memories of January 1974 when our kids were nine, six, and three. I had just transferred to Atlanta and Edie was a single parent – selling the house (and clearing the driveway of Syracuse's record snowfall so buyers could come in and make insulting offers). As Jennifer listened to Edie reminisce, she said she finally understood the significance of that Rolling Stones classic, "Mother's Little Helper."

We're getting ready to host the whole clan this Christmas. All three kids, spouses, and grandchildren will come over the river and through the woods on December 19th to test the capacity of grandmother's house. Actually, we'll spend the first few days at an Episcopal Retreat Center in the North Carolina mountains, where grandmother need neither cook nor clean. Margaret and Kenny will join us there for what we expect will be a relaxing holiday getaway. Maybe a little snow?

Grandmother's house has undergone extensive renovation this year. Edie grilled a gazillion contractors, painters and carpet people – references, background checks, drug tests – you can never be too careful.... I have sat on every sofa and club chair between Macon and the Tennessee border; and the paint colors are now narrowed down to Brass Ingot, Candlestick, Cherry Pink, and Apple Blossom White. The wall is gone between the kitchen and family room; we've discarded the back issues of Southern Living from 1986 through 1998; and we've thrown out the three old TV sets we were saving just in case that newfangled cable and remote control thing didn't catch on. Plus, Al Gore promised us a new deck and screened porch during his token campaign stop in Georgia, so y'all come see us next spring.

May God bless you this season as he has blessed us,

The Cobourns
110 Canter Court
Roswell, GA 30076-1013
Christmas, 2001

Merry Christmas,

Last year – after the date by which Edith and I *would* have mailed the Christmas letter had we not been fighting – we welcomed our children and their families from the west coast. Edith and I were fighting over the Christmas letter. This war is part of what defines our holiday spirit. Normally, we kiss and make up in time to compromise on the text of our annual epistle and perpetuate the charade that we are an adorable and functional couple to whom quirky things happen.

Not last year.

Since my life is a series of rigid, self-imposed deadlines, I usually start the war around Labor Day, asking Edith if she has finished her entries for the Christmas letter. When Edith completes that task in her own time – often around the third Sunday in Advent – the battle begins over the inclusion of her spiritual reflections vs. my highly embellished memories. Last year's war ended in a cease-fire that came too late for a timely mailing.

Christmas itself was peaceful and fulfilling, however. We spent four days with Kenny and Margaret and our children and grandchildren at Kanuga, an Episcopal retreat in the North Carolina mountains. We had cold snow, hot cider, boisterous family meals, horse and carriage rides, magic shows, caroling, and naps for the grands (-children and -parents). Christopher loved the buffet lines where he could pick out his own meals (pancakes, hash browns, bacon, and a notable absence of such politically correct provisions as granola and tofu sausage, which is what people from California eat). Edith has found her favorite way to host large family gatherings – at a site where somebody else cooks the meals, makes the beds, and cleans up the spilled Gummy Worms. The snow stayed on the ground through Christmas day at our house, so the little ones unwound from opening presents by making snow balls and snow angels, and tracking in mud just like their parents used to do.

In the meantime, Jennifer had come up with a creative way to honor Edith's 60th birthday. She asked a number of Edith's friends to contribute a card describing their relationship and a bead symbolic of that connection. In late January, Jen mailed two big boxes full of beads and cards, along with an album for the cards and cord for the beads. Edie spent an emotional couple of days reading the testimonies and stringing the beads – heartwarming reminders of friends near and far.

In the spring, Liz swam, ran, and biked through another Seattle triathlon. This time, she coerced Shannon into participating with her. Next year, Shannon thinks she will run the beer concession at the end of the race instead. Shortly after the triathlon, both Liz and Shannon announced they were pregnant, reinforcing my long-held belief that that much exercise can't possibly be good for you. This will be Shannon's first, Liz's second, and our fifth. Shannon's will arrive around December 15. Liz's will arrive around January 1. Edith will arrive on January 4.

My banjo and I took a week-long frailing course at the Campbell Folk School in North Carolina in March. The instructor, David Brose, is an archivist and historian who, in addition to being an expert banjo player, has done a lot of field recordings throughout the Appalachians since the 70's. His stories of the authentic musicians and old timey music were as valuable to me as the banjo lessons themselves.

He told us one day of a local craftsman who had been making unusual historical instruments for over fifty years – hurdy-gurdies and tabor-pipes as well as recorders and dulcimers. George was a feisty old curmudgeon with strong opinions about everything, especially banjos. George hated banjos. ("Ze best plaze for a benjo iss a tresh ken.") David's wife had a dulcimer she had bought from George when she was sixteen. When she took it in many years later for repair, George eyed it with disdain.

"Zis iss a pieze of crep! Look et de vorkmenzhip! Dizguzting!"

"Why, George, I bought this from you in 1970."

"But maybe I ken fix up a leedle."

In June, we headed northwest to celebrate Andy's graduation from the Art Institute of Seattle. His degree is in mixed media and he is currently designing websites as a freelancer. He and Shannon are hoping to relocate to the southeast sometime, and were back in October hunting for houses and jobs. For now, though, they've subdivided their spare bedroom into an office/nursery/guest room. We got a tour during our Thanksgiving visit and were cautioned to be careful where we stepped or we'd be out of the nursery and into the office. "Ooops! Now you're in the guest room again!" Shannon is on maternity leave and they are both eagerly awaiting the arrival of "Peanut."

Nurse Liz is working three shifts a week in the mother/baby unit of Providence Hospital in Seattle. Little Sam is two and is adorable, Liz says, except when he is biting little girls in his daycare center. He loves the men – his uncles and gompas – but takes a little longer to warm up to the women. We're sure he'll soon learn that you're supposed to bite the boys and love the girls. Jason has just taken a new sales job and he and Liz are hoping to move to a new house on Bainbridge Island, where Jason grew up. This will mean commuting by ferry. Sounds kinda neat to us (riding on a ferry, that is; not going to work)!

Meanwhile, Jen and Ray are content in sunny southern California where they added a backyard pool this summer. Christopher, at seven, could already swim, and four year-old Anna was doggie paddle safe within a few weeks. Ray has been back and forth to Hong Kong this year, looking after his older brother who is losing his battle with cancer. Christopher has joined the children's choir at church, but Jennifer reports that he has not yet captured the angelic reverence of the group. He sings a few notes, but gets quickly distracted – by the adult to his left who is signing the words for the deaf; by the little girl to his right who is poking him to behave; and by his parents who are cringing in the third pew. As if merely observing Christopher's behavior weren't bad enough, the children recess to sit with their families after the performance, so the entire congregation can now match Christopher with his obviously unfit parents.

Edith spends as much time as possible on our new screened porch. The porch is the end of the second phase of the redecorating project we began early last year: repainting and recarpeting upstairs, opening up and brightening the living room, and replacing the old deck. Last December found us furiously painting alongside the painter, struggling to get the inside work done before the kids arrived. Phase II, the porch and deck began in January and were *finally* complete in June. Remodeling! Yuccchh! It might just be easier to move. But the porch is worth all the agony. It's Edith's tree house. She says it feels just like a summer cottage. Now all she needs is a lake in the backyard...... Phase III is the kitchen and dining room and Phase IV is the entire downstairs. (My heart is beginning to fibrillate as I type this. I'm afraid Phase V will be either bankruptcy, death, or, if I'm *really* unlucky, assisted living.)

This project was a very spiritual experience for Edith, and she could never have survived it without the help of Chris, a decorator friend from church. Edie had never really redecorated much before since IBMers don't remodel; they relocate. She followed the example of her mother – who altered and hung the same curtains in every house they lived in, and rearranged the same furniture to fit whatever space was available. Edith's mother could have moved to Kabul and had the cave sparkling within a week.

I think the redecorating project is a natural extension of her renewed interest in the arts. She's taken several courses over the past few years, but the interest was really stimulated by a program called "The Artist's Way," a concept of expressing your life in art rather than words. The process was important, not the product, and the process was incredibly revealing. She has continued with art therapy this year and has found she expresses herself best in "mixed media." Unlike Andy's definition of mixed media, hers is "making things out of junk." Or as our late folk artist, Howard Finster, said, "I took the peaces you trew away, and put them together by nite and day. Shaped by the rain, dried by the sun, a million peaces are in one."

Edie has also found a new outreach activity at Holy Comforter Church in southeast Atlanta. She answered an ad in the Diocesan newspaper for a van driver. (**"VAN DRIVER!"** I cried, remembering her frequent auto mishaps.) Luckily, they put her in the art room.

Holy Comforter ministers to the mentally ill who live in nearby group homes. Edith wears a STAFF nametag every Tuesday so no one is tempted to put her on the bus at the end of the day.

One of her favorites is John, a very shy young man who told her one day about a funeral he had attended recently. John twirls his hair as he talks, head cast down, glancing upward through the tops of his eyes from time to time.

"Well, how was the funeral, John?"

"Oh, it was OK. OK. (twirl, twirl) Right in the middle I had to take a pee and a poop. I guess that wasn't too good, was it, Edith."

The art room's goal is recovery ... at some level ... and recovery is slow. One of the participants, Patricia, makes clay faces week after week. At Halloween, Edith dressed her in a kimono and a headband with two bouncy coils on top – the only things left in the costume box. "Patricia, you look beautiful," Edith told her, "Take a look at yourself in the bathroom mirror!"

She returned with her arms outstretched and a glowing smile on her face. "I'm an angel," she exclaimed. "I'm an *angel!*"

What Edith had dismissed as a mismatched costume had clothed a beautiful, dark-skinned, gap-toothed angel – smiling and holding her arms out to us all.

"And suddenly, there was with the angel a multitude of the heavenly host, praising God and saying, "Glory to God in the highest, and on earth, peace, good will toward men.

Love and blessings to you and your angels this holy season.

The Cobourns
110 Canter Court
Roswell, GA 30076-1013
Christmas, 2002

Happy Holidays,

The stock market is down, but the census in the Cobourn family is up: two new Seattle-born boys came three weeks apart – Jed Cobourn on December 20 (10 lbs. 4 oz.), and Henry Joss on January 10 (8 lbs. 15 oz.)! No small feats!

All three kids came home for visits this summer and one family stayed. Andy and Shannon have moved to Jasper, about 45 minutes north of us, and we are thrilled to be able to see them without having to get on Delta first. Andy is working as a graphic artist and Shannon is cleaning up after Jed. Jed is a drooler. We've been threatening to get a Saturday Night Live drool cup to hang around his neck. Producing the pre-talking sounds he makes apparently requires massive amounts of saliva. It's a little like having a banana slug for a grandson.

Andy and Shannon are glad to be back in the southeast, but they've experienced some culture shock moving from urban Seattle to rural Georgia. No longer able to buy láttes, free-range tofu and organic Hershey bars, they are now surrounded by Confederate flags and sorghum mills. Shoppers at the local Piggly Wiggly look at Jed and tell Shannon, "He shore is a big ole boy, ain't he?" They could swear they've moved from Nancy Pelosi's district to Trent Lott's.

Jason and Liz moved to a new house on Bainbridge Island in the spring – a 30-minute ferry ride from the city – prompting Edith and Jennifer to plan a Seattle summer vacation. One of the 50 things Edith most desparately wanted to do before she died was to get out of Atlanta in August. Mission accomplished. We found a wonderful house on the beach and explored all of Liz's favorite playgrounds and forest trails. The grandchildren's favorite event was fishing with Uncle Jason. This is not to say that fishing was Uncle Jason's favorite event, as he soon learned that Sam and Anna do not yet have the patience that serious fisherpersons require. The kids did better fishing off the deck where they caught their limit of ferns.

Sam, at three, is the Question King who hardly needs anyone to converse with.

"We goin' fishin', Grampy?"

"Yes, Sam."

"Why we goin' fishin', Grampy?"

"To eat some fish, Sam."

"I like fish, Grampy."

"So does Grampy, Sam."

"Why I like fish, Grampy?"

While we were on Bainbridge, Henry and Christopher were baptized. Christopher had been indignant two years earlier at Sam's christening when he realized he himself had not yet been sprinkled and sealed. ("You shoulda had *me* baptized, Mom!") So we took care of "bidness." We could have made *three* new Christians, but Anna demurred. Instead, she helped the priest with the water (Jordan River water that Edith had brought back from Israel in '94). Christopher interceded on the way home, though. Carrying the baptismal shell the priest had given him, he scooped up some rainwater and asked Anna if she wanted to be baptized now. This time the answer was yes. "I don't know all the words, so this will be a mini-baptism," he said, pouring a few drops down her forehead and onto her beaming smile. To borrow the title of one of Edith's favorite movies: this ... is *As Good As It Gets*. We had to rush Henry's christening gown home for Jed's baptism before he outgrew it.

We spent Thanksgiving in L.A. with the Tse's, arriving on Thursday to a Southern California Thanksgiving feast: tamales and yams. Anna had a hot dog. Edie took cello lessons from Christopher ("Twinkle, Twinkle, Little Star") and played golf with Ray. Now she wants golf lessons for Christmas so she can participate with her sons. ("Don't leave Grammy at home! I want to go out and play, too!")

Edie's spiritual side took a new twist this year. She has become very interested in the peace movement. It began with a conference she attended entitled "Islam and Christianity – Is there a way forward?" and continued with Episcopal Peace Fellowship meetings. She doesn't think I've quite caught the same spirit. On the way to her first meeting last January, I asked if they'd be going to the Atlanta airport to stick flowers in the rifles of the National Guardsmen. She promised to suggest it to the group.

Meanwhile, I had a really heartwarming 62nd birthday in October. These are some of the birthday wishes you get from your family when they think you're too old to retaliate: "To discover if you're really old, look to the East. Did your neck hurt when you turned your head?" "Enjoy your birthday while you still can." "I didn't get you a funny card. I know how easily people your age pee in their pants."

I had what turned into a semi-serious medical adventure in February – sinus surgery. According to my doctor, the one with the bedside manner of a brussel sprout, it was just routine. "Ah, just outpatient stuff – an hour or so in recovery and you'll be good as new." (The recovery room nurse said, "You *may* feel some discomfort when you try to actually breathe, Mr. Cobourn, but that'll go away in just a few days.") Well, the infection could not all be treated surgically, so the *routine* turned out to be intravenous anti-biotics for six weeks – two hours in the morning and two hours in the evening. Dr. Sprout had forgotten to warn Edith that she would be administering the IV's at home through the pic line in my arm. Now I had to watch her carefully to make sure she didn't inject air into my veins. And as if that weren't stressful enough, one of the medicines dropped my white blood count so low that I had to take neupogen shots for a week. I didn't really see the shimmering light, but I do sort of remember floating above my chair, watching Edith read over the insurance policy. Being housebound with such an affliction makes one particularly sensitive to all the medical ads on TV, especially ones that feature people my age cavorting through fields of heather. ("Premicor! Take control of your life! Common side effects may include splitting headaches, hearing loss, and spastic colon. Ask your doctor if Premicor is right for you!")

Edie joined a Habitat work crew recently to help build a house for one of the artists at the Holy Comforter Friendship Center. Jerome's house is only the third ever built for a person with a mental illness – a new venture for Habitat. Edie has two *very* bruised fingers to show for her novice status with the hammer, but she achieved a tremendous feeling of accomplishment as she swung the doorframe she had built into place. She can't wait to go back – as soon as her fingernails grow out again.

By fall, she had just enough energy left for a trip to New York with Peggy Hayes. They did the plays, visited Ellis Island, and rode the ferry past Miss Liberty. But the highlight was a visit to St. Paul's at Ground Zero – the church that opened its doors to all who helped with the 9/11 rescue and recovery efforts, 24 hours a day for nine months. Countless artifacts and photographs throughout the church narrate the stories of those heroic people and the hundreds of volunteers who came to help – podiatrists, massage therapists, counselors, cooks, musicians, clergy.

"I was overwhelmed by the evidence of God's presence, even in the face of such horror," Edie said. "I saw and heard the Christmas story come to St. Paul's day after day after day. There's a verse of 'Oh Little Town of Bethlehem' that we sang recently which seems to reinforce what I saw:"

Where children pure and happy/pray to the blessed child
Where misery cries out to thee/son of the Mother mild
Where charity stands watching/and faith holds wide the door
The darkness wakes, the glory breaks/and
Christmas comes once more.

Looking back over 2002, the incredible Bainbridge Island vacation stands out. As we sat in the swing on our last night, gazing at the Seattle skyline across the sound, it all seemed too magical. We wondered to each other how we ended up here – married almost forty years, blessed with wonderful children and children-in-law and granchildren. (I remembered that Chuck Bell is always quick to point out that he's been married almost forty years, too ... albeit to three different women.) Then some broken clouds passed over the Space Needle. It seemed to be blinking. I was reminded of Meg Ryan's line in *Sleepless in Seattle*. She mused that it wasn't magic, "It was a sign!"

But it *was* magic. Our life has been magic. Sure, it seemed like just a shell game from time to time, but on the whole, even as we move gracefully toward closure.....

"I have had a *very* good life," I thought, "progressing from hunter-gatherer to nursing home company executive." Edie is my nurturer, my spiritual director, and my agent for change. She is an otter – playful and tireless. And I have chronicled our time together in 30 years' worth of letters – our Christmas greetings seasoned with growth spurts and reflections, triumphs and foibles. And, of course, magic.

I turned toward Edith on the swing.

> "It *has* been magic, hasn't it, honey – as magical as David ... um ... whatsisname."
> "Who?"
> "You know. David, the magician ... um ... starts with a "C.""
> "Oh, yes; I know. It isn't David."
> "Yes it is! I know it is! Oh, Jeez, David ... Ca ... Ce ... Ci ... Co ... uh ... Coa ... you know, the guy Dan watched who made the Statue of Liberty disappear."
> "It's not David."

Anyway, we remember to send our blessings and prayers to you this season,

p.s. It is *too* David

CPSIA information can be obtained at www.ICGtesting.com
Printed in the USA
LVOW050311050912

297345LV00002B/18/A

9 781594 670169